CONTENTS

INTRODUCTION

for a couple of years, I'd been sitting on the idea of working on a book with the Henry Glass designers, but it wasn't until October 2012, at the International Quilt Market in Houston, that we actually talked more seriously about the possibility. I was dining with Jill Finley and the rest of the Henry Glass crew when the conversation suddenly turned to this very suggestion: What about a book with designs by the Henry Glass designers? At that moment, I knew it was time to put the book together.

We had Hurricane Sandy on our minds that day. My flight home, scheduled for the next day, had been cancelled, but I managed to rebook and get out on the last flight. My family survived the storm with little effect, but many more families along the East Coast suffered hardships when their homes and property were severely damaged or destroyed.

The storm put a new perspective on things, and soon after Quilt Market, the book started to evolve. I contacted my editor at Martingale, Karen Burns, about the idea. She and the editor in chief, Mary Green, jumped to back the proposal. My fellow Henry Glass designers followed with their unanimous and enthusiastic support. I am grateful to them all.

I couldn't have asked for a better group of individuals to work with. The Henry Glass CEO, Robert Fortunoff, leads the way with his strength, vision, and passion for his family business. Company president, Larry Reichenberg, provides the leadership to put out an awesome product, and design directors Karen Junquet, Harriet Clemens, and Lisa Loessel make us all look great.

The fabulous Henry Glass designers have created some equally fabulous projects for this book using Henry Glass fabrics. The best thing is that they have donated their work, and all royalties from this book will be donated to the Red Cross.

I thank everyone for their generosity and commitment to this worthy project.

Best,

LINDA LUM DEBONO

Delightful

MEET JACQUELYNNE STEVES

When I'm making a quilt, I like to see the patterns that emerge as the blocks are joined together. For this reason, I prefer a lot of contrast in my fabric choices. It might be contrast between two colors such as blue and orange, or the play of yellow against an all-white background. Another trick to turn up the contrast in your quilts is to incorporate solids or tone-on-tone fabrics. "

Want the emphasis to be on the blocks and shapes created where they come together? Contrast between fabrics is the key. Using mottled or nearly solid prints helps the other prints stand out. —Jacquelynne Steves

Delightful
Designed, pieced, and appliquéd by
Jacquelynne Steves; quilted by Daniela Durham
Finished quilt size: 55½" x 55½"
Finished block size: 9" x 9"

Materials

Yardage is based on 42"-wide fabric.

1½ yards of orange tone on tone for scallops, flowers, inner border, and binding
1½ yards of white tone on tone for blocks and flowers
1 yard of blue print for blocks
⅞ yard of floral print for outer border
⅝ yard of yellow tone on tone for scallops
½ yard of green tone on tone for scallops
¼ yard of green polka dot for flowers
3½ yards of fabric for backing
61" x 61" piece of batting
Paper-backed fusible web
Template plastic

Cutting

From the orange tone on tone, cut:
5 strips, 1½" x 42"
6 strips, 2¼" x 42"

From the white tone on tone, cut:
4 strips, 9½" x 42"; crosscut into 16 squares, 9½" x 9½"

From the blue print, cut:
3 strips, 9½" x 42"; crosscut into 9 squares, 9½" x 9½"

From the floral print, cut:
6 strips, 4½" x 42"

Preparing the Appliqués

1 Trace the scallop and flower patterns on page 9 onto template plastic and cut on the solid lines. The patterns have been reversed for fusible appliqué.

2 Trace 100 scallops and nine of *each* flower template onto the paper side of the fusible web, leaving at least ¼" between shapes.

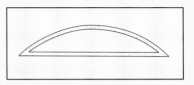

REDUCE BULK

To reduce the bulk and stiffness of the fusible web used in this project, cut out the center of each fusible-web scallop, following the dashed line on the pattern. When fusing, work from the center of the arc toward the edges to prevent distortion of the shape.

Start fusing at center;
slowly work toward ends.

3 Roughly cut out the traced shapes to separate them.

4 Following the manufacturer's instructions, fuse each scallop to the wrong side of the appropriate fabrics to make 48 orange, 28 yellow, and 24 green tone-on-tone scallops.

5 Fuse each flower piece to the wrong side of the appropriate fabrics to make nine large white flowers, nine green polka-dot small flowers and nine orange flower centers.

6 Cut out the appliqués on the traced lines. Peel away the paper backing.

Making the Blocks

Stitch all pieces with right sides together and a ¼" seam allowance unless otherwise noted.

1 Referring to the illustrations below for color placement, place four scallops (adhesive side down) on each blue or white 9½" square, aligning the straight edges. Fuse the scallops in place to secure. Label the blocks A, B, C, D, and E as indicated.

Block A.   Block B.   Block C.   Block D.   Block E.
Make 9.   Make 4.   Make 4.   Make 4.   Make 4.

2 Using a zigzag, blanket, or other machine stitch, appliqué the curved edge of each scallop in place with matching thread. Leave the straight edges unstitched.

3 Fuse a large white flower to the center of each blue block, varying the flower's rotation in some blocks. Appliqué with white thread. Layer a small green flower on top of each white flower, rotating the petals as shown. Fuse the flower in place and appliqué with green thread. Fuse an orange flower center in place and appliqué with orange thread.

Assembling the Quilt

1 Referring to the quilt assembly diagram, sew the blocks into five rows of five blocks each, noting the scallop-color placement. Press the seam allowances open.

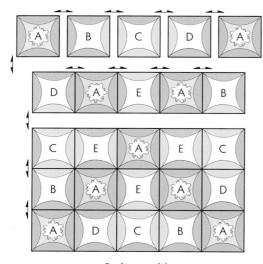

Quilt assembly

2 Join the rows to complete the quilt top. Press the seam allowances open.

PRESSING MATTERS

Press the seam allowances open instead of to one side. This will better distribute the bulk of the fusible web, making the seams flatter and easier to sew across.

Adding the Borders

These border measurements have been calculated mathematically, but the actual size needed for your quilt may vary. Measure across the width and length of your quilt and cut your borders to size. For more information, visit ShopMartingale.com/HowtoQuilt for free instructions on quiltmaking techniques.

1 Remove the selvages and sew the five orange 1½"-wide strips together end to end, using diagonal seams, to make a long strip. Crosscut the long strip into two strips, 45½" long, and sew them to the top and bottom of the quilt. Press the seam allowances toward the inner border.

2 Crosscut the remaining long strip into two strips, 47½" long, and sew them to the sides of the quilt. Press the seam allowances toward the inner border.

3 Remove the selvages and sew the six floral strips together end to end, using diagonal seams, to make a long strip. Crosscut the long strip into two strips, 47½" long, and sew them to the sides of the quilt. Press the seam allowances toward the outer border.

4 Crosscut the remaining long strip into two strips, 55½" long, and sew them to the top and bottom of the quilt. Press the seam allowances toward the outer border.

Finishing the Quilt

For more information on finishing techniques, visit ShopMartingale.com/HowtoQuilt.

1 Cut the backing fabric into two equal lengths. Remove the selvages and sew the pieces together along a lengthwise edge.

2 Layer the quilt top, batting, and backing. Baste the layers together. Hand or machine quilt as desired. The quilt shown was machine quilted in the ditch around the appliqué shapes and with 1" crosshatching in the white backgrounds of the blocks without flowers. The orange scallops feature straight lines spaced 1" apart, and a feather motif was quilted in the inner border.

3 Trim the backing and batting even with the quilt top, squaring up the quilt sandwich.

4 Bind the quilt using the orange 2¼"-wide strips. Add a hanging sleeve, if desired, and a label.

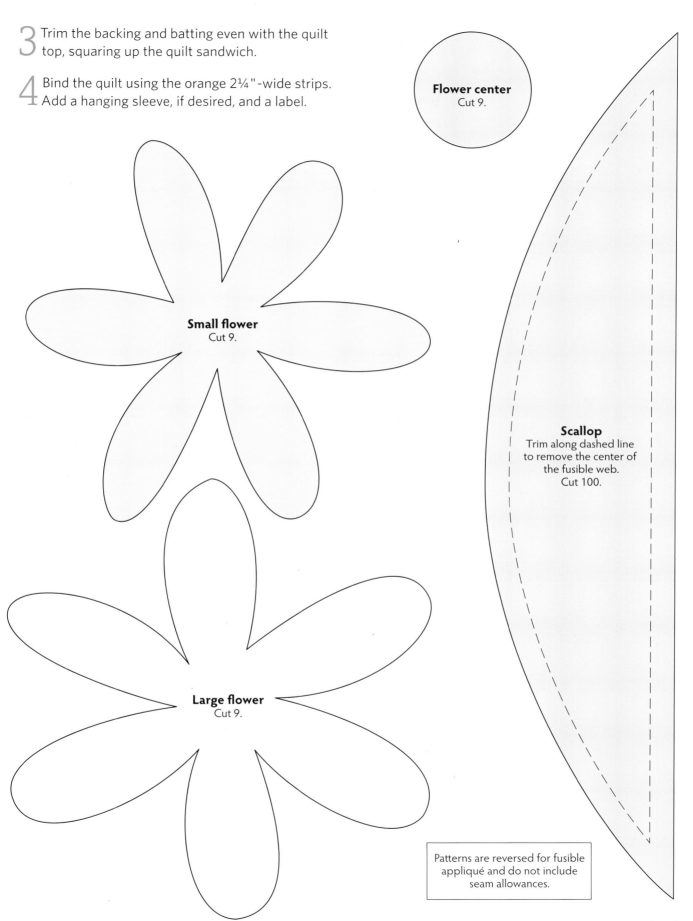

Flower center
Cut 9.

Small flower
Cut 9.

Large flower
Cut 9.

Scallop
Trim along dashed line to remove the center of the fusible web.
Cut 100.

Patterns are reversed for fusible appliqué and do not include seam allowances.

MEET HEATHER MULDER PETERSON

My approach to designing fabric is pretty simple. I always begin by working on the focus print in the collection. In my case, I love starting with a large-scale floral (or something more whimsical, like a fish print) that includes nearly all of the colors that are part of the overall palette. Once that's complete, I add the coordinates that are essential in making a quilt interesting—all in a variety of scales, including florals, geometrics, tonals, dots, and more. Often I'll include a stripe for interest.

The "Funky Flowers" quilt illustrates this progression, from the large floral used for the vase to the stripe on the binding and everything in between.

It's the same way I decorate my home. I start with a focal item that has all the colors I want to use, such as a rug or pillow. Then I pull coordinates, using the focal item as a guide. "

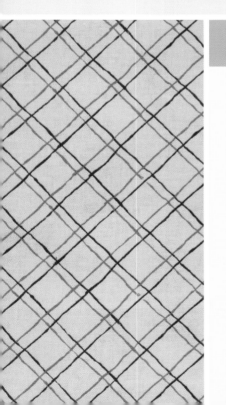

Take a Cue From Your Wardrobe

You can easily translate my approach to designing a fabric collection into choosing fabrics for your quilts.

Too many people think of selecting fabrics as a daunting task. Most of us don't really think about the fact that we're all cultivating fabric and color combinations every day when we get dressed. Choosing the main pieces for an outfit is no different than selecting one or two key prints for a quilt. Accenting those choices with accessories that add a little splash of color or wearing a bold piece of jewelry to give your your outfit a little sparkle is similar to adding a pop of color to be used sparingly in a quilt top.

Choosing and mixing fabrics you love in a quilt is something I'm confident you can do!

Funky Flowers
By Heather Mulder Peterson of
Anka's Treasures

Finished quilt size: 24¼" x 33¾"

Materials

Yardage is based on 42"-wide fabric.

⅝ yard of gray print for background*
⅝ yard of multicolored stripe for binding
    and appliqué
¼ yard of brown print for inner border
¼ yard of cream print for outer border
Assorted scraps of yellow, green, blue, and brown
    prints for outer border and appliqués
⅞ yard of fabric for backing
29" x 39" piece of batting
1¼ yards of ½"-wide green rickrack

*If you choose a directional print, you will need ⅞ yard of
fabric to cut the background on the lengthwise grain.*

Cutting

From the gray print, cut:
1 rectangle, 18" x 27½"

From the brown print, cut:
2 strips, 1¼" x 19½"
2 strips, 1¼" x 27½"

From the cream print, cut:
2 strips, 3¼" x 42"; crosscut into 22 squares,
    3¼" x 3¼"

From the assorted scraps, cut:
22 squares, 3¼" x 3¼"

From the multicolored stripe, cut:
1 square, 19" x 19"; cut into 2½"-wide bias strips
    totaling 140" in length

Preparing the Appliqués

Using the patterns on pages 14 and 15, prepare the
appliqués for your chosen method; the sample quilt
features fusible appliqué with zigzag and blanket-
stitch edges. The patterns are reversed for fusible

*Create a custom look in the perfect
palette for your decor—a vase of playful
blooms surrounded by an easy-to-create
zigzag border. It's a fuss-free way to
brighten any room.*

—Heather Mulder Peterson

appliqué. Visit ShopMartingale.com/HowtoQuilt
for free, downloadable instructions for a variety of
appliqué techniques.

You will need one each of the vase bottom, vase
top, vase band, flower A, and flower A center; two
each of flower B, flower B center, flower C, and
flower C swirl; and six leaves.

Appliquéing the Quilt Center

1 Referring to the quilt photo on page 10, arrange
    and layer the appliqué shapes on the gray
rectangle. Pin or baste in place. Don't fuse yet.

2 Cut lengths of green rickrack to make the
    five stems, adding ½" at each end for seam
allowance. Position the rickrack on the appliqué
layout, tucking the ends behind the flowers and the
vase top, and pin or baste in place.

3 Stitch through the center of each rickrack
    stem using a straight stitch and matching
thread. Stitch the edges of each appliqué piece as
desired. Heather used a machine blanket stitch.

Adding the Borders

Stitch all pieces with right sides together and a
¼" seam allowance unless otherwise noted.

1 Sew the brown 1¼" x 27½" strips to the sides of
    the quilt and press the seam allowances toward
the inner border. Sew the brown 1¼" x 19½" strips
to the top and bottom of the quilt. Press the seam
allowances toward the inner border.

2 Draw a line diagonally from corner to corner
    on the wrong side of each cream square. Place
a marked square on a print square, right sides

together, and sew ¼" from each side of the drawn line. Cut on the drawn line and press the seam allowances toward the print triangle to make two half-square-triangle units. Make 44.

Make 44.

3 Referring to the quilt assembly diagram below, join 12 half-square-triangle units to make a side border, placing matching prints together and orienting the units to produce the zigzag pattern. Press the seam allowances in one direction. Make two. Sew an assembled border to each side of the quilt. Press the seam allowances toward the inner border.

4 Join 10 half-square-triangle units, pairing matching prints and orienting the units as shown, to make a top/bottom border. Press the seam allowances in one direction. Make two. Sew the assembled borders to the top and bottom of the quilt. Press the seam allowances toward the inner border.

Finishing the Quilt

1 Cut the backing fabric to measure 6" longer and wider than the quilt top. Layer the quilt top, batting, and backing. Baste the layers together. Hand or machine quilt as desired. The quilt shown features a large feather motif in the brown vase, allover swirls in the gray background, and meander quilting in the light-print triangles of the border.

2 Trim the backing and batting even with the quilt top.

3 Bind the quilt using the striped 2½"-wide bias strips. Add a hanging sleeve, if desired, and a label.

Quilt assembly

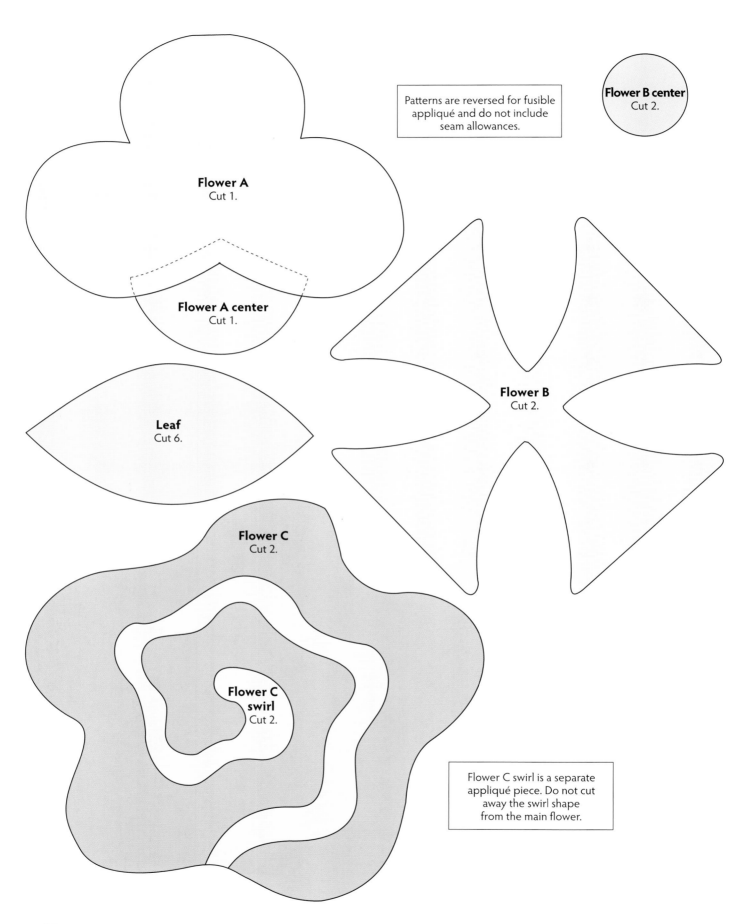

Patterns are reversed for fusible appliqué and do not include seam allowances.

Flower B center
Cut 2.

Flower A
Cut 1.

Flower A center
Cut 1.

Flower B
Cut 2.

Leaf
Cut 6.

Flower C
Cut 2.

Flower C
swirl
Cut 2.

Flower C swirl is a separate appliqué piece. Do not cut away the swirl shape from the main flower.

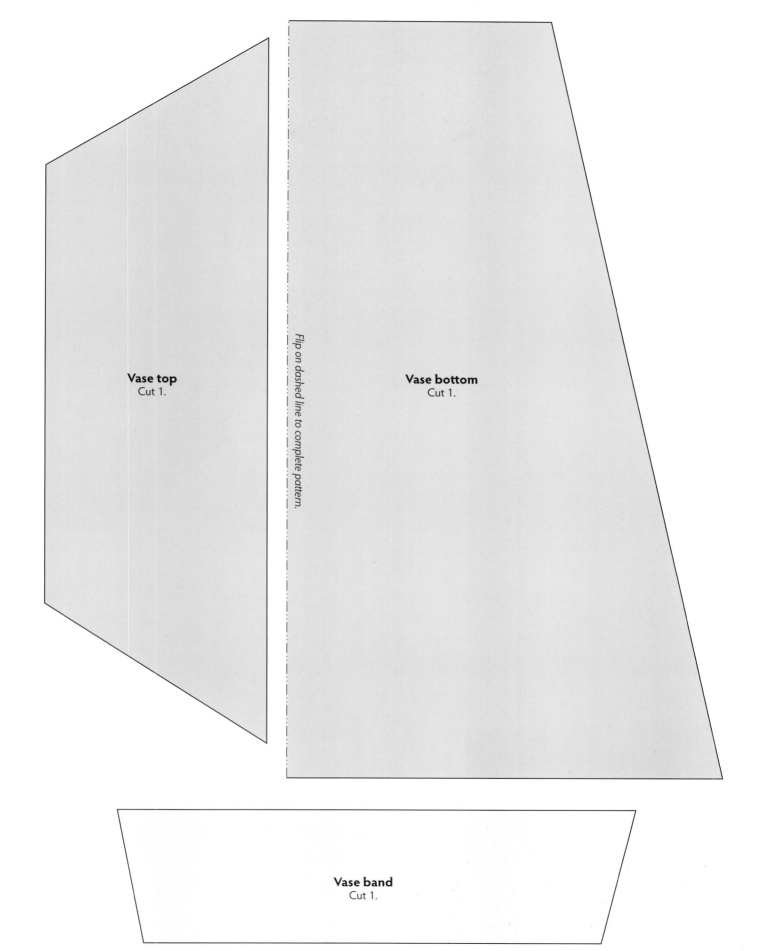

Vase top
Cut 1.

Flip on dashed line to complete pattern.

Vase bottom
Cut 1.

Vase band
Cut 1.

Making a Plan for Leftovers

A common refrain among quilters, whether they collect fat quarters or buy yardage without a project in mind, often sounds like this: "I'm not sure how much I'll need of any one fabric, so I buy almost equal amounts of all. But, then I'm left with pieces that supported the main print and don't know how to use them once the main print is gone."

Sound familiar? Well your flair for fabric mixing and matching is about to improve! On this page (and five more like it—pages 27, 33, 43, 50, and 61), you'll find real-life solutions from an avid quilter (and former quilt-shop owner), Jan Ragaller, for using those remainder fabrics in another project by mixing in a variety of other prints. For each exercise, she'll show you a fabric range from a single collection— much like what you might buy in a bundle of designer Heather Mulder-Peterson's fabrics at right. The second photo (below left) removes a couple prints from the original palette and replaces them with a couple new prints (not from the same collection or designer) to steer the assortment in another direction.

And more than just seeing the new combinations, you'll learn the secrets to why the additional fabrics were selected. It all adds up to an arsenal of color- and print-selecting ideas that will help you develop a flair for choosing great fabric combinations for your next project.

Original fabric collection

Deconstructing the Details

Finding another large-scale print that incorporates all the colors of the remainder prints you have isn't always easy, but think of it as a treasure hunt. In this case, there are three medium-scale prints left over. A patchwork bird-and-flower print pulls in the color palette from the three existing blender fabrics, giving the palette a new focal print. Notice the colors don't have to match exactly. *Close* counts when choosing fabrics, and the slight variations make the overall mix more interesting. Keying in on the blue dots in the brown polka dot and the blue in the focal print, adding a small-scale turquoise tone-on-tone print increases the variety in scale, while keeping with a vibrant hue to balance out the strong orange and green prints.

Secondary fabric assortment

Blueberries and Bananas Place Mats

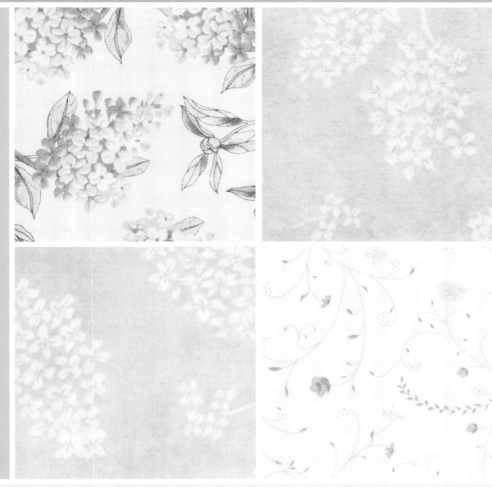

MEET VICKI OEHLKE

" *I need not look further* than the flower garden when finding inspiration for my fabrics. I begin with a large floral that might include peonies or roses—flowers with many soft, gorgeous petals. I balance that with a viney floral that has smaller flowers, buds, berries, or tiny leaves. Add in a soft plaid and I've got the beginnings of a fantastic fabric line. "

If you're stuck trying to pick a mix of fabrics for a project, look at the assortment in a quilt you love. Is it all small prints? Or is there a large-scale floral, a small floral, and a solid? Choose a comparable mix of prints and patterns to replicate the effect.

—Vicki Oehlke

Blueberries and Bananas Place Mats
Designed and pieced by Vicki Oehlke of WillowBerry Lane

Finished place-mat size: 13½" x 19½"

Materials

Yardage is based on 42"-wide fabric and is sufficient for four place mats.

⅝ yard of white print for piecing
⅝ yard of red print for piecing and binding
½ yard of blue print for piecing

½ yard of yellow print for piecing
1¼ yards of fabric for backing
32" x 44" piece of batting

Cutting

From the yellow print, cut:
24 squares, 3⅞" x 3⅞"

From the blue print, cut:
24 squares, 3⅞" x 3⅞"
8 rectangles, 1½" x 3½"

From the white print, cut:
48 squares, 3½" x 3½"
16 rectangles, 1½" x 3½"

From the red print, cut:
4 squares, 1½" x 1½"
16 rectangles, 1½" x 3½"
8 strips, 2" x 42"

From the fabric for backing, cut:
4 rectangles, 16" x 22"

From the batting, cut:
4 rectangles, 16" x 22"

Assembling the Place-Mat Fronts

Stitch all pieces with right sides together and a ¼" seam allowance unless otherwise noted.

1 Draw a diagonal line from corner to corner on the wrong side of each yellow square. Place a marked yellow square on a blue square, right sides together, and sew ¼" from each side of the drawn line. Cut on the drawn line and press the seam allowances open to make two half-square-triangle units. Make 48.

Make 48.

2 Divide the white, red, and blue rectangles and squares and the half-square-triangle units into four groups. Arrange the pieces from one group as shown in the photo on page 18 and the place-mat assembly diagram below, noting the orientation of each half-square-triangle unit.

3 Sew the units in each row together. Press the seam allowances in odd rows toward the center of the place mat; press the seam allowances in even rows away from the center.

4 Join the rows to complete the place-mat front. Press the seam allowances in one direction. Make four.

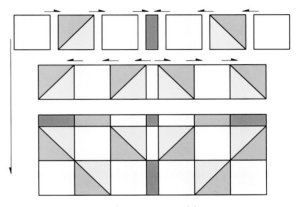

Place-mat assembly.
Make 4.

Finishing the Place Mats

1 Layer a place-mat front with batting and a backing rectangle. Baste the layers together. Hand or machine quilt as desired.

2 Trim the batting and backing even with the place-mat top. Repeat to layer, quilt, and trim all four place mats. The place mats shown were machine quilted in the ditch.

3 Bind the place mats using the red 2"-wide strips.

MEET LINDA LUM DEBONO

I start designing with a theme—it could be the alphabet, flowers, or even a trendy color combination. I love all colors but mostly bright and happy colors which include lime, yellow, orange, fuschia, turquoise, and red. Some people might be surprised to learn I also like basics such as black, gray, and blue. Though it might seem contradictory, those basics provide a nice balance to the brights.

Designing a collection with just the right mix of coordinates is tricky, because ideally you'd like to include prints that can be used for different purposes such as binding or sashing. The scale of prints is also important. Even though my specialty is appliqué, others might use the fabric for piecing quilts or making garments or accessories. I try to keep those variables in mind as I create.

Variety Can Be the Spice

How many fabrics should a quilt have? There isn't a perfect number, but I'd say that I habitually use as many as possible.

I once made a quilt that ended up with 15 to 20 different fuschia prints in it. It wasn't an accident. I was purposeful in my decision to make the quilt super scrappy. The reason is this: By designing that way, I'm not always tied into using a single print. Consequently, I'm not so stressed if I run out of a particular fabric. I know there will always be other options I can mix in. Also, I think by using a large variety of fabrics the project really pops in the end.

Try it. The more the merrier. I think you'll find there's a certain freedom that comes from scrappy.

I step back and look at my projects on a design wall through a reducer. That way I can see any weak area or tone down overpowering spots. —Linda Lum DeBono

Close to My Heart
Designed and made by
Linda Lum DeBono
Finished pillow size: 20½" x 20½"

Materials

Yardage is based on 42"-wide fabric, except where noted. Fat quarters measure 18" x 21".

⅝ yard of white tone on tone for pillow front
6 rectangles, 2" x 4", of assorted green prints for leaves
1 fat quarter of black polka dot for ribbon
⅝ yard of muslin for lining
Assorted 5" squares or scraps of pink, red, yellow, blue, and orange prints for appliqués
⅞ yard of orange print for pillow back
¼ yard of black print for binding
22" x 22" piece of batting
1 yard of lightweight fusible web
18" pillow form*

*Using a smaller pillow form gives the project a relaxed, under-stuffed appearance. Use a 20" pillow form if you prefer a fuller look.

Cutting

From the white tone on tone, cut:
1 square, 22" x 22"

From the muslin, cut:
1 square, 22" x 22"

From the orange print, cut:
1 rectangle, 20½" x 24"
1 rectangle, 20½" x 26"

From the black print, cut:
3 strips, 2¼" x 42"

Preparing the Appliqués

Using the patterns on pages 24–26, prepare the appliqué pieces shown in the chart below for your chosen method; the sample pillow features fusible appliqué with zigzag-stitched edges. Remember to reverse the patterns if you are using fusible web for the appliqués.

Visit ShopMartingale.com/HowtoQuilt for free, downloadable instructions for a variety of appliqué techniques.

Shape	Quantity
Leaf	10
Flower A	2
Flower B	5
Flower C	5
Flower C center	5
Flower D	2
Flower D center	2
Flower E	1
Flower E center	1
Heart A	5
Heart B	1
Bow, sections 1–4, and bow knot	1 *each*

Appliquéing the Pillow Front

1 Referring to the pillow photo on page 20 and the illustration on page 23, arrange and layer the flowers, hearts, leaves, and bow appliqués on the

white 22" square in a heart shape. Exact placement isn't essential, but keep the shapes within a 20" x 20" design area.

Appliqué placement

2 Fuse, and then stitch each appliqué shape to the white square.

Quilting the Pillow Front

1 Layer the muslin square, batting square, and appliquéd pillow front, matching their centers, and pin to secure.

2 Quilt the pillow front as desired. The pillow shown was quilted with an allover motif in the white background areas.

3 Trim the quilted pillow front to measure 20½" x 20½".

Assembling the Pillow

1 Fold and press the orange 20½" x 24" rectangle in half, wrong sides together, to measure 20½" x 12". Fold and press the orange 20½" x 26" rectangle in half, wrong sides together, to measure 20½" x 13".

2 Place the orange pillow back pieces on the wrong side of the pillow front with the folded edges overlapping in the center, matching the raw edges of the front and backs. Baste around all four sides to secure.

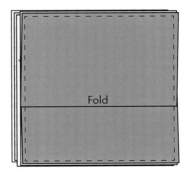

Fold

Overlap folded edges in center.

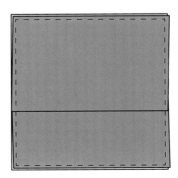

3 Bind the pillow edges using the black 2¼"-wide strips. Insert the pillow form.

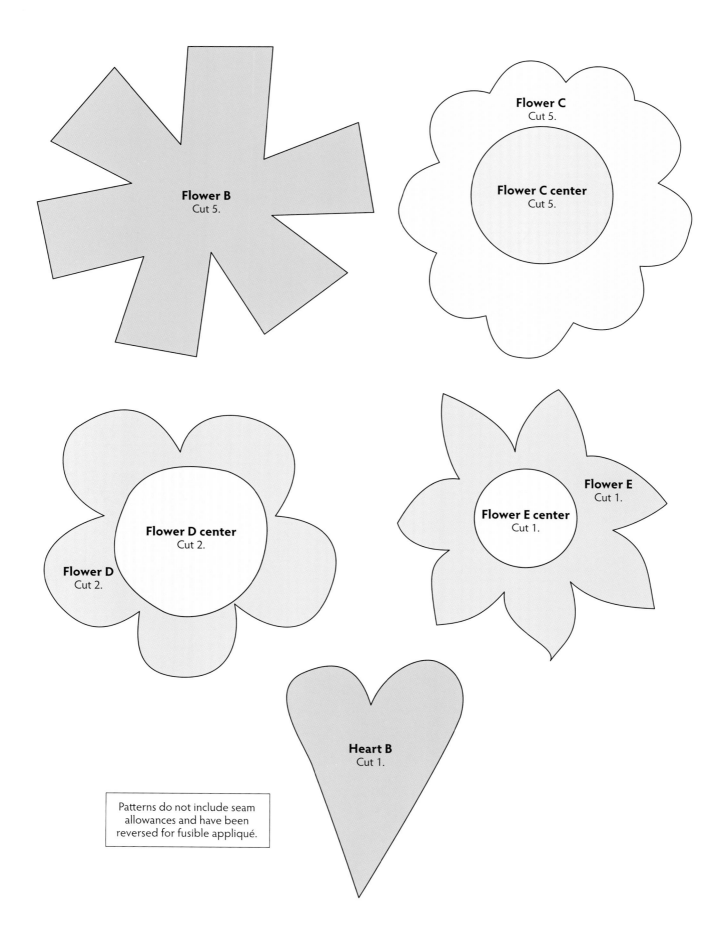

Flower B
Cut 5.

Flower C
Cut 5.

Flower C center
Cut 5.

Flower D center
Cut 2.

Flower D
Cut 2.

Flower E
Cut 1.

Flower E center
Cut 1.

Heart B
Cut 1.

Patterns do not include seam allowances and have been reversed for fusible appliqué.

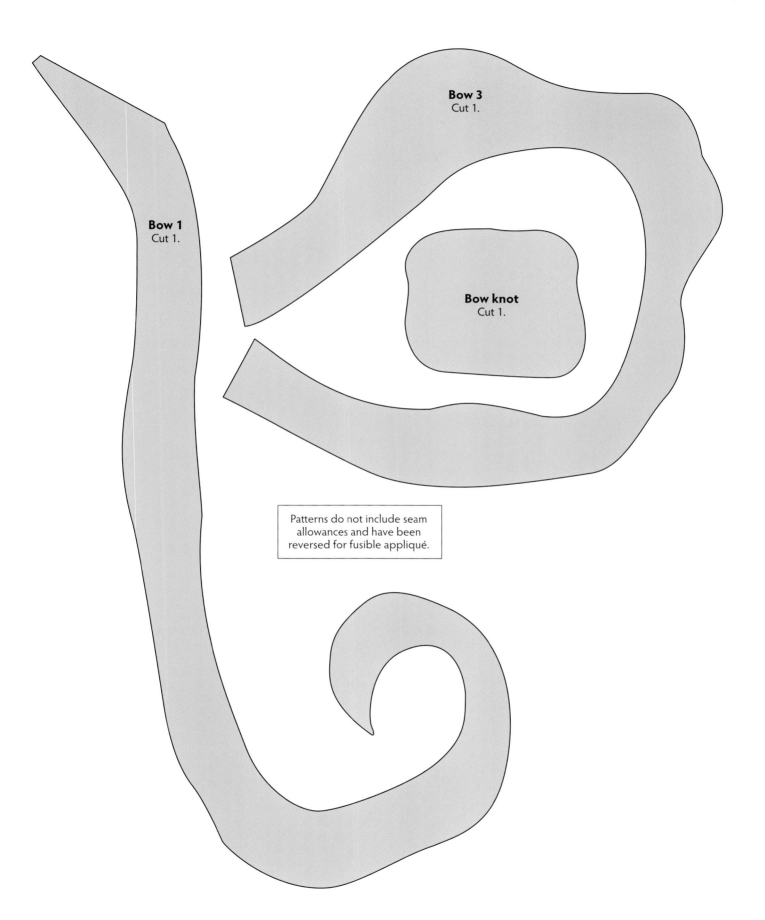

Bow 3
Cut 1.

Bow 1
Cut 1.

Bow knot
Cut 1.

Patterns do not include seam
allowances and have been
reversed for fusible appliqué.

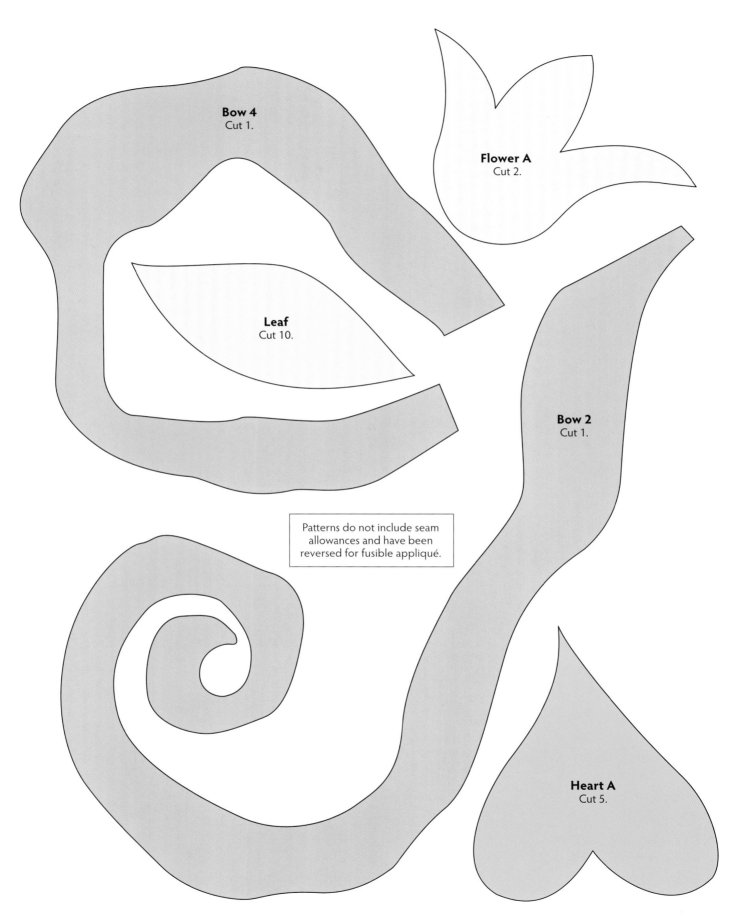

Bow 4
Cut 1.

Flower A
Cut 2.

Leaf
Cut 10.

Bow 2
Cut 1.

Patterns do not include seam allowances and have been reversed for fusible appliqué.

Heart A
Cut 5.

Cream and White and Stripes, Oh My!

A pair of dark-brown prints provides a perfect foil for the contrasting brights in the original fabric collection from designer Linda Lum DeBono. But what you might miss at first glance is the subtle mix of both cream and white in the prints. A few flower petals, the center stripe, and Xs in the XOXO all have stark white, contrasting with the cream background of the plaid print. Quilters sometimes think of cream and white as an either/or proposition, but this collection proves otherwise. Cream and white can be an either/*and* choice!

Deconstructing the Details

What's the solution for fabrics that remain from a project when they all seem to match so closely that introducing something from outside the collection seems impossible? As illustrated by the two fabrics across the top of the secondary fabric assortment below, the common element they share is lime green. Short of adding more lime prints, what's a quilter to do?

The large print added to the mix has a few things that help integrate into a new palette: print scale (the new grouping needed something larger), color (more variety, but still a hint of lime), and an element of stripes, too (check out a few of the flower stems). The dark areas in the large print also provide some balance to the grouping overall. Without it, the remaining dark-brown floral print would stand out too much.

Original fabric collection

The blue in the new large print also provides the basis for introducing the blue-and-white print, which repeats a geometric element with its stripe-like design. Don't be afraid to use more than one stripe in a project. The results can be fun when you look for different scales, repeats, and colors. Consider, too, whether to alternate the direction of stripes in a quilt or keep them all parallel.

Secondary fabric assortment

27

MEET LITTLE QUILTS

Decorating magazines that featured antique doll quilts displayed on walls, in baskets, or other settings inspired Alice Berg, Sylvia Johnson, and me to begin our business, Little Quilts. At the time, the quilts shown were too expensive for most people to purchase, so we started making kits with reproduction fabrics from our stashes so quilters could make their own versions.

Inspired by those antique quilts, we replicated the balance of small, medium, and large prints with coordinating background fabrics of tone-on-tone and shirting prints. Those same principles guide the designs of our fabric collections as well. Although we try to create in a variety of color palettes to suit differing tastes, we endeavor to select colors that will complement one another when they're put together in a quilt.

Fun is the Goal—Make Do!

Too often, too many quilters get caught up in looking for the "perfect " fabric or making sure every point is perfectly stitched. We want quilters to have fun making Little Quilts and not worry about perfection. Let the fabrics wow the viewer.

In our estimation, the "perfect" number of fabrics in a quilt is . . . more. In other words, there are never too many fabrics when they coordinate well with one another.

Making blocks with several different shades of a single color is key, substituting fabrics that are almost, but not quite, the same. Doing so mimics the look of many an antique quilt where the quiltmaker was forced by circumstances to make do with what she had on hand.

We like each fabric collection to have lights, mediums, and darks, as well as a varied scale of design, because those are the same attributes we're looking for when we pull fabrics to make a quilt. —Little Quilts

Days Gone By

Designed by Mary Ellen Von Holt,
Alice Berg, and Sylvia Johnson of Little Quilts

Finished quilt size: 28" x 36"

Materials

Yardage is based on 42"-wide fabric.

⅝ yard *total* of assorted light scraps for blocks
and setting triangles

⅝ yard *total* of assorted medium scraps for blocks
and setting triangles

½ yard of lengthwise blue stripe for border

⅜ yard of blue print for border

¼ yard of dark-brown print for sashing

⅓ yard of red print for binding

1 yard of fabric for backing

33" x 41" piece of batting

Cutting

From the assorted light scraps, cut:

112 squares, 1½" x 1½"

6 squares, 5½" x 5½"; cut into quarters diagonally
to yield 24 triangles

4 squares, 3½" x 3½"; cut in half diagonally to yield
8 triangles

From the assorted medium scraps, cut:

140 squares, 1½" x 1½"

6 squares, 5½" x 5½"; cut into quarters diagonally
to yield 24 triangles

4 squares, 3½" x 3½"; cut in half diagonally to yield
8 triangles

From the dark-brown print, cut:

3 strips, 2" x 42"

From the blue print, cut:

3 strips, 3½" x 42"

From the blue stripe, cut *on the lengthwise grain*:
1 strip, 3½" x 14"
1 strip, 3½" x 12"
1 strip, 3½" x 10"

From the red print, cut:
4 strips, 2¼" x 42"

Making the Blocks

Stitch all pieces with right sides together and a ¼" seam allowance unless otherwise noted.

1 Sew one light square between two medium squares to make segment A. Press the seam allowances toward the darker squares. Make 56.

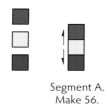

Segment A.
Make 56.

2 Sew one medium square between two light squares to make segment B. Press the seam allowances toward the center square. Make 28.

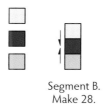

Segment B.
Make 28.

3 Sew one B segment between two A segments to make a Nine Patch block. Press the seam allowances toward the B segments. Make 28 blocks.

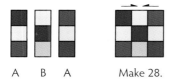

A   B   A   Make 28.

Assembling the Quilt

1 Arrange seven blocks and six medium and six light setting triangles in seven short diagonal rows. Sew the units in each row together and press the seam allowances toward the setting triangles.

2 Join the rows to make a panel. Sew two medium corner triangles and two light corner triangles to the top and bottom of the panel. Press the seam allowances in one direction. Trim the edges, leaving a ¼" seam allowance beyond the seamline intersections. Make four panels.

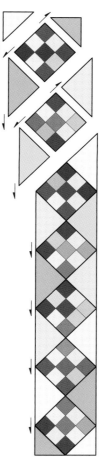

Panel assembly.
Make 4.

3 Measure the length of the block panels. Average the measurement and trim the three dark-brown sashing strips to match the average measurement.

4 Sew the four block panels and three sashing strips together to complete the quilt top. Press the seam allowances toward the sashing strips.

Adding the Border

1 Sew the blue-print strips together end to end to make a long strip. Crosscut the strip into four strips, 30" long.

2 Sew the striped 14"-long strip to a blue-print 30"-long strip to make the border for the quilt's left edge. Trim the side border to the average panel measurement from step 6 of "Assembling the Quilt" including 11½" of the striped strip. Sew the border to the left edge of the quilt and press the seam allowances toward the border.

3 Sew the striped 12"-long strip to a second blue-print 30"-long strip to make the right border. Trim the pieced border to the average panel measurement, including 8¾" of the striped strip. Sew the border to the right edge of the quilt and press the seam allowances toward the border.

4 Sew the striped 10"-long strip to a third blue-print 30"-long strip to make the bottom border. Measure the width of the quilt top through the center, including the side borders, and trim the bottom border to that measurement, including 6¾" of the striped strip. Sew the border to the bottom of the quilt and press the seam allowances toward the border.

5 Trim the remaining blue-print 30"-long strip to the quilt-width measurement and sew it to the top of the quilt. Press the seam allowances toward the border.

Finishing the Quilt

1 Cut the backing fabric 6" longer and wider than the quilt top. Layer the quilt top, batting, and backing. Baste the layers together. Hand or machine quilt as desired. The quilt shown was hand quilted. The Nine Patch blocks were quilted with straight lines through the centers of each dark square, while the vertical sashing and borders were quilted with meandering vines.

2 Trim the backing and batting even with the quilt top.

3 Bind the quilt using the red 2¼"-wide strips. Add a hanging sleeve, if desired, and a label.

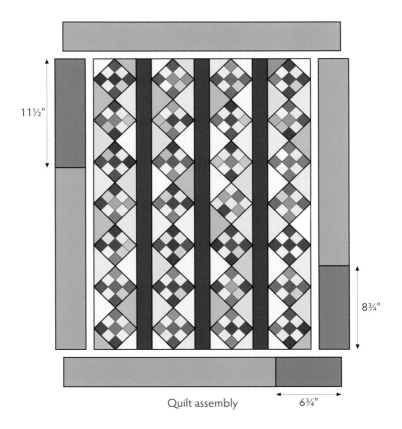

11½"

8¾"

Quilt assembly

6¾"

Opposites Attract Attention

Mid-tone, medium-sized prints are the bread-and-butter of many a quilt and many a quiltmaker's stash. As with this pleasing palette of Little Quilts prints (right), the medium zone may include a range of colors with limited diversity in tones. But staying in the medium zone, while safe and satisfying, doesn't mean you can't veer off into lights and darks occasionally. Adding in both ends of the spectrum on either side of the mid-tones increases the contrast and provides a vivid alternative. Check out the secondary palette below.

Deconstructing the Details

Contrast in color isn't the only way opposties attract. Gone are the days when quilters had "rules" about what they could or couldn't mix together in a quilt. Today, quilters are encouraged to consider the possibilities of mixing cotton prints, batiks, lawn cottons, and more—all in a single project.

Don't limit your mid-tone, medium-scale prints to combining only with other fabrics of the same type. They will easily work together with stronger prints. By adding batiks to the two remaining fabrics (shown in the secondary fabric assortment below), the new assortment takes on a different attitude.

Original fabric collection

A deliberate choice to add starkness in color and prints is made with the selection of two batiks—introducing a light cream and a dark teal—to contrast with the mid-tone medium-scale floral. The dark-blue design found in the teal batik is the noticeable tie to the small-scale navy print that rounds out the range, bringing the darkest element to the mix. The result is a light-to-dark palette that makes use of a couple medium remainder prints in a higher contrast assortment.

Try these tips to stretch your fabric leftovers or stash in new directions.

Secondary fabric assortment

MEET JILL FINLEY

Designing fabric is very personal to me. When I start my work on a collection, the seed of the idea often begins with something that I feel connected to—such as a favorite flower or a treasured handwritten letter. Ultimately, quilters using the fabric may never know just what that inspiration was, but having identified it at the outset helps me create.

I love the look of fresh, new modern florals in a larger scale for big blocks and borders. But sometimes the most important pieces in a group are the small-scale tonals, because they're what I use for appliqué.

When choosing fabrics for a quilt, I audition them on a design wall, adding or taking away until I get the desired mix. For a look that's less "flat" and often results in a more interesting quilt, consider making blocks with different prints in the same color. "

Discover Your Go-To Color

Most of us have a color muse. It may be a self-proclaimed favorite color you find everywhere in your wardrobe and in nearly every room of your house. Or it could be a striking, saturated color that you use sparingly, but pops of it are well-placed in your accessories or home-decor accents. Even if you don't use it in every quilt, your sewing room wouldn't be without it! I often use red or black in my quilts. Red is bright and cheerful, and black provides high contrast.

Identifying your color muse might help you add that special spark to your next quilt. Including a little or a lot of it is your choice—but consider including at least a dash of the color you love most! Make it your signature.

Breezy
Designed, pieced, and appliquéd by Jill Finley
of Jillily Studios; quilted by Maika Christensen
Finished quilt size: 86½" x 86½"
Finished block size: 12" x 12"

Materials

Yardage is based on 42"-wide fabric.

3¾ yards of white polka dot for blocks and borders

2½ yards of green floral for blocks and border

1¾ yards of black print for vines, borders, appliqués,
  and binding

1⅝ yards of blue polka dot for borders

⅝ yard of green tone on tone for appliqués, blocks,
  and pieced border

½ yard of blue tone on tone for appliqués and blocks

½ yard of blue print for pieced border

¼ yard of black polka dot for blocks

⅛ yard of green check for appliqués

7¾ yards of fabric for backing

92" x 92" piece of batting

Freezer paper

Fabric glue such as Appli-Glue

½" bias-tape maker (optional)

Cutting

From the black print, cut:
1 rectangle, 20" x 42"; cut into 8 bias strips, 1⅛"
  wide. Reserve the remainder for appliqués.
13 strips, 1½" x 42"
9 strips, 2¼" x 42"

From the white polka dot, cut:
48 squares, 2½" x 2½"
8 squares, 3" x 3"
10 squares, 4" x 4"
4 squares, 4½" x 4½"
10 squares, 5½" x 5½"
4 squares, 6½" x 6½"
32 rectangles, 1½" x 4½"
16 rectangles, 2½" x 4½"
48 rectangles, 2½" x 6½"
30 rectangles, 3½" x 6½"
12 strips, 1½" x 42"
5 strips, 4½" x 42"

From the green floral, *cut on the lengthwise grain:*
2 strips, 6½" x 70½"
2 strips, 6½" x 82½"
16 squares, 3½" x 3½"
10 squares, 4" x 4"

From the black polka dot, cut:
20 squares, 2" x 2"
16 rectangles, 2½" x 4½"

From the green tone on tone, cut:
16 squares, 2¼" x 2¼"
10 squares, 5½" x 5½"

From the blue tone on tone, cut:
8 squares, 3" x 3"

From the blue print, cut:
80 squares, 2½" x 2½"

From the blue polka dot, cut:
5 strips, 5½" x 42"
9 strips, 2½" x 42"

Preparing the Appliqués

1 Using the patterns on page 42, prepare 60 blue
  tone-on-tone petals, four blue tone-on-tone
circles, eight black-print leaves, eight black-print
reversed leaves, eight green-check leaf highlights,
and eight green-check reversed leaf highlights for
your chosen appliqué method. The sample quilt
features hand appliqué using freezer paper and glue
basting. Reverse the patterns if you are using fusible
web for the appliqués.

Visit ShopMartingale.com/HowtoQuilt for free,
downloadable instructions for a variety of appliqué
techniques.

2 Press ⅜" of each long edge of a black bias strip
  to the wrong side to form the vine strips. Or
use a ½" bias-tape maker to turn the long edges of
the vine strips to the wrong side quickly and easily.
You'll use two strips on each side of the quilt front.

Making Block A

Stitch all pieces with right sides together and a ¼" seam allowance unless otherwise noted.

1 Draw a line from corner to corner on the wrong side of each white polka-dot 4" square. Place a marked square on a green-floral 4" square, right sides together, and sew ¼" from each side of the drawn line. Cut on the drawn line and press the seam allowances open to make two half-square-triangle units. Trim each unit to measure 3½" x 3½". Make 20.

Make 20.

2 Draw a line from corner to corner on the wrong side of each black polka-dot 2" square. Place a marked square on the top-right corner of a white polka-dot 3½" x 6½" rectangle as shown, right sides together, and sew on the drawn line. Trim the excess corner fabric ¼" from the sewn line and press the seam allowances toward the corner to make unit 1. Make 10.

3 Place a marked square on the bottom-right corner of a white polka-dot 3½" x 6½" rectangle. Sew on the drawn line. Trim the excess corner fabric ¼" from the sewn line and press the seam allowances toward the corner to make unit 2. Make 10.

Unit 1.
Make 10.

Unit 2.
Make 10.

Creating a scrappy quilt with fabrics from many collections is a favorite look of mine. It's fun to mix and match lots of fabrics. —Jill Finley

4 Sew two of each unit together to make a block center. Make five.

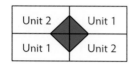

Make 5.

5 Sew a white polka-dot 3½" x 6½" rectangle between two half-square-triangle units from step 1, orienting the half-square-triangle units as shown. Press the seam allowances toward the rectangle. Make 10.

Make 10.

6 Sew units from step 5 to the top and bottom of a block center. Press the seam allowances toward the block center. Make five.

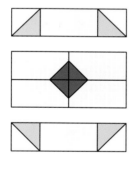
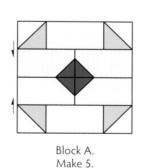

Block A.
Make 5.

7 Arrange 12 petals around the central black square of one block A and stitch the petals to the block. Leave the rounded end of one petal free for inserting the end of the vine later; see the quilt assembly diagram on page 41 for placement.

Making Block B

1 Draw a line from corner to corner on the wrong side of each green tone-on-tone 2¼" square. Place a marked square on one corner of a white polka-dot 4½" square, right sides together, and sew on the drawn line. Trim the excess corner fabric ¼" from the sewn line and press the seam allowances toward the corner.

2 Add triangle corners to the remaining three corners of the white square in the same way to make a square-in-a-square unit. Make four.

Make 4.

3 Draw a line from corner to corner on the wrong side of each white polka-dot 3" square. Place a marked square on a blue tone-on-tone 3" square, right sides together, and sew ¼" from each side of the drawn line. Cut on the drawn line and press the seam allowances open to make two half-square-triangle units. Make 16.

Make 16.

4 Sew a white polka-dot 2½" square to the top of a half-square-triangle unit from step 3, orienting the unit as shown. Press the seam allowances toward the square. Sew a white polka-dot 2½" x 4½" rectangle to the left side of the unit and press the seam allowances toward the pieced unit.

5 Draw a line from corner to corner on the wrong side of each green-floral 3½" square. Place a marked square on the top-left corner of a pieced unit from step 4 as shown. Sew on the drawn line. Trim the excess corner fabric ¼" from the sewn line

and press the seam allowances toward the resulting triangle to make a corner unit. Make 16.

Make 16.

6 Draw a line from corner to corner on the wrong side of each remaining white polka-dot 2½" square. Place a marked square on the left end of a black polka-dot 2½" x 4½" rectangle as shown. Sew on the drawn line. Trim the excess corner fabric ¼" from the sewn line and press the seam allowances toward the corner.

7 Repeat step 6 to add a marked square to the right end of the rectangle, making a flying-geese unit.

8 Sew white polka-dot 1½" x 4½" rectangles to the top and bottom of the flying-geese unit to make a side unit. Make 16.

Make 16.

9 Arrange four side units, four corner units, and one square-in-a-square unit as shown. Sew the units together in rows, pressing the seam allowances as shown. Join the rows to complete block B. Press the seam allowances toward the center row. Make 4.

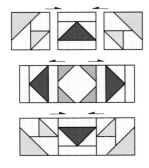 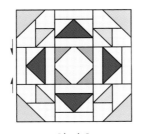

Block B.
Make 4.

Assembling the Quilt

1 Arrange the A and B blocks in three rows of three blocks each, alternating the blocks in each row. Sew the blocks together in rows. Press the seam allowances in alternating directions from row to row.

2 Join the rows to make the quilt center. Press the seam allowances in one direction.

Making the Pieced Border

1 Draw a line from corner to corner on the wrong side of each white polka-dot 5½" square. Place a marked square on a green tone-on-tone 5½" square, right sides together, and sew ¼" from each side of the drawn line. Cut on the drawn line and press the seam allowances open to make two half-square-triangle units. Make 20.

Make 20.

2 Draw a diagonal line from corner to corner, perpendicular to the seam, on the wrong side of 10 units from step 1. Place a marked unit on an unmarked unit, alternating the color placement and

matching the seams. Sew ¼" from each side of the drawn line. Cut on the drawn line and press the seam allowances open to make two hourglass units. Trim each unit to measure 4½" x 4½". Make 20.

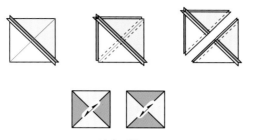

Make 20.

3 Draw a diagonal line from corner to corner on the wrong side of each blue-print 2½" square. Place a marked square on the left end of a white polka-dot 2½" x 6½" rectangle as shown. Sew on the drawn line. Trim the excess corner fabric ¼" from the sewn line and press the seam allowances toward the corner.

4 Repeat step 3 to add a marked square to the right end of the same rectangle, but press the seam allowances toward the white rectangle. Make 32.

5 Sew two units together, orienting the triangles as shown, to make a border unit. Press the seam allowances to one side. Make 16.

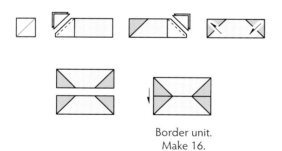

Border unit.
Make 16.

6 Place a marked square from step 3 on the left end of a white polka-dot 2½" x 6½" rectangle as shown. Sew on the drawn line. Trim the excess corner fabric ¼" from the sewn line and press the seam allowances toward the corner to make unit A. Make eight.

7 Repeat step 6, changing the orientation of the line, to make unit B. Press the seam allowances toward the rectangle. Make eight.

8 Sew a unit A to each unit B as shown to make a border end unit. Press the seam allowances to one side. Make eight.

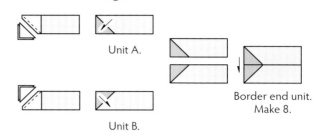

Unit A.

Unit B.

Border end unit.
Make 8.

9 Sew the white polka-dot 1½" x 42" strips together end to end to make a long strip. Crosscut the long strip into eight strips, 56½" long.

10 Join five hourglass units, four border units, and two border end units as shown. Press the seam allowances to one side.

11 Sew white polka-dot 1½" x 56½" strips to the top and bottom of the pieced unit to make a border panel. Press the seam allowances toward the white polka-dot strip. Make four.

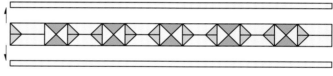

Make 4.

Adding the Inner Borders

After sewing each border strip to the quilt center, press the seam allowances toward the newly added border.

1 Sew the white polka-dot 4½" x 42" strips together end to end to make a long strip. Crosscut the long strip into two strips, 36½" long, and two strips, 44½" long. Sew the 36½"-long strips to the top and bottom of the quilt center. Sew the 44½"-long strips to the sides of the quilt center.

2 Sew the blue polka-dot 5½" x 42" strips together end to end to make a long strip. Crosscut the long strip into two strips, 44½" long, and two strips, 54½" long. Sew the 44½"-long strips to the top and bottom of the quilt. Sew the 54½"-long strips to the sides of the quilt.

Appliquéing the Quilt

1 Referring to the quilt photo on page 37 and the quilt assembly diagram below, arrange the black bias strips to create the stems. Place the circles over the stem ends and position the leaves and leaf highlights as shown. Jill likes to glue baste the appliqués in place.

2 Stitch the appliqués to the quilt by hand or machine. Jill appliquéd the sample quilt by hand.

Adding the Outer Borders

After sewing each border strip to the quilt center, press the seam allowances toward the newly added border.

1 Sew the black-print 1½" x 42" strips together end to end to make a long strip. Crosscut the long strip into two strips, 54½"-long, and two strips, 56½" long. Sew the 54½"-long strips to the top and bottom of the quilt. Sew the 56½"-long strips to the sides of the quilt. Crosscut the remaining long strip into two strips, 68½"-long, and two strips, 70½"-long. Set these strips aside for the fifth border.

2 Sew two pieced border panels to the top and bottom of the quilt center. Sew a white polka-dot 6½" square to each end of each remaining border panel. Press the seam allowances toward the squares, and then sew these panels to the sides of the quilt.

3 Sew the black-print 68½"-long strips to the top and bottom of the quilt. Sew the black-print 70½"-long strips to the sides of the quilt.

4 Sew the green-floral 6½" x 70½" strips to the sides of the quilt. Sew the green-floral 6½" x 82½" strips to the top and bottom of the quilt.

5 Sew the blue polka-dot 2½" x 42" strips together end to end to make a long strip. Crosscut the long strip into two strips, 82½"-long, and two strips, 86½"-long. Sew the 82½"-long strips to the sides of the quilt. Sew the 86½"-long strips to the top and bottom of the quilt.

Quilt assembly

Finishing the Quilt

1 Cut and piece the backing fabric so it is 6" longer and wider than the quilt top.

2 Layer the quilt top, batting, and backing. Baste the layers together. Hand or machine quilt as desired. The quilt shown was machine quilted with swirls in the white background areas, straight lines ¾" apart in the blue areas, and a large feather motif in the wide green border.

3 Trim the backing and batting even with the quilt top, squaring up the quilt sandwich.

4 Bind the quilt using the black-print 2¼"-wide strips. Add a hanging sleeve, if desired, and a label.

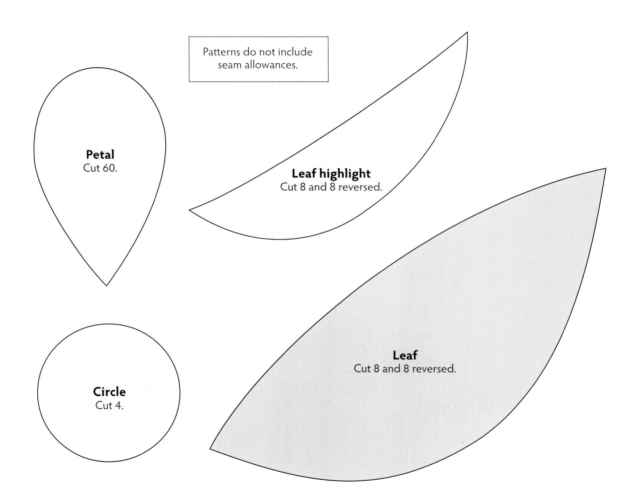

Patterns do not include seam allowances.

Petal
Cut 60.

Leaf highlight
Cut 8 and 8 reversed.

Circle
Cut 4.

Leaf
Cut 8 and 8 reversed.

More than many other types of collections, floral groupings seem to center on their stunning large-scale prints as the launching point for other supporting prints in the grouping, as illustrated in designer Jill Finley's original collection at right. That's often what makes these collections so appealing to quiltmakers. Everything seems to fit together perfectly, like a well-designed garden.

Deconstructing the Details

Much like a garden at season's end, what do you do when most of the flowers are gone in a floral collection you've purchased? Get creative! The secondary assortment shown below focuses on the limited color range of the remainder fabrics. The remaining bold chevron and airy black-and-white print called for dense and concentrated colors to round out a new group. The remaining fabrics also needed an additional print that bridged the colors and introduced new ones to the palette.

The green random dot is a great option that does just that! Repeating the green of the zigzag print, it also brings yellow, blue, and pink into the mix. From there, a whimsical black floral print repeats the secondary colors and adds a dark, bold print to the array. Finally, a small white dot on a butter-yellow field adds a nice medium-tone print that's colorful but not overpowering. Voilà, a new garden already planting the seeds for another quilt.

Original fabric collection

Secondary fabric assortment

Garden Bramble

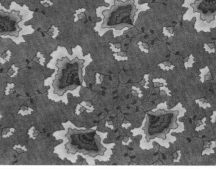

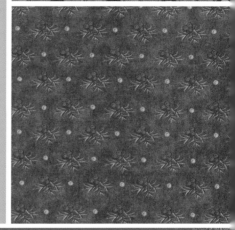

MEET KIM DIEHL

❝*I have a little confession to make:* I am a fabriholic with a serious addiction to scrap quilts! With this in mind, my approach when I design my fabric collections is to put together groups of prints and colors that work well together, but don't look as though they were created together. As a new quilter, I discovered that taking the scrappy approach to selecting fabrics made it easy to be successful, and modeling my fabric collections in this way makes it easy for others to be successful, too. For quilts where I'm working from "scratch" and gathering a ton of different fabrics, my favorite method of auditioning them is to toss the prints I'm considering into a random pile on the floor, take a step back, and look at the blend. If I find myself questioning whether I like the mix, I listen to that little voice inside and make changes. When I love what I see, I trust my instincts, grab my rotary cutter, and dive into my project.❞

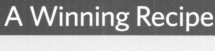

A Winning Recipe

When I began designing for Henry Glass, I took a really objective look at the quilts I've stitched through the years and realized that I instinctively use a "formula" when choosing my fabrics—floral and geometric prints of varying scale, something that reads as a stripe, and a mix of prints with both vintage and modern elements. This recipe guides me as I design my collections, and when I draw from a core group of colors it enables the fabrics to be interchangeable from line to line. With this approach, the prints from each collection take away the guesswork and . . . voilà! Instant scrap quilt!

Garden Bramble

Designed, pieced, and machine appliquéd by
Kim Diehl; machine quilted by Deborah Poole

Finished quilt size: 50½" x 60½"

Finished block size: 10" x 10"

Materials

Yardage is based on 42"-wide fabric, except where noted. Fat quarters measure 18" x 21" and fat eighths measure 9" x 21".

1¾ yards of medium-light neutral print for blocks and border

¾ yard of dark-blue print for flower centers and binding

½ yard of light-neutral print for blocks

½ yard of red print for flowers

10 fat quarters of assorted prints for blocks, berries, and border

1 fat quarter of green stripe or print for vines and leaves

2 fat eighths of assorted green prints for leaves

1 fat eighth of gold print for stars

3¼ yards of fabric for backing

56" x 66" piece of batting

Liquid fabric glue, water-soluble and acid-free

My favorite look mixes simply pieced patchwork backgrounds with meandering appliqués that cross over the block intersections. It creates an interesting finished quilt that leaves you wondering how it all came together. —Kim Diehl

Cutting

Reserve scraps for appliqués.

From the green stripe or print, cut:
1½"-wide bias strips totaling at least 100" in length

From the assorted prints, cut a *total* of:
26 squares, 3½" x 3½"
24 squares, 5½" x 5½"
48 squares, 3" x 3"
10 squares, 5⅞" x 5⅞"; cut in half diagonally to yield 20 triangles

From the medium-light neutral print, cut:
13 squares, 10½" x 10½"
10 squares, 5⅞" x 5⅞"; cut in half diagonally to yield 20 triangles

From the light-neutral print, cut:
48 squares, 3" x 3"

From the dark-blue print, cut:
6 strips, 2½" x 42"

Preparing the Appliqués

1 Using the patterns on pages 48 and 49, prepare 7 red flowers, 7 dark-blue flower centers, 11 gold stars, 15 assorted-print berries, 11 assorted-green large leaves, 6 green-striped small leaves, and 9 assorted-green small leaves for your chosen appliqué method. The sample quilt uses the freezer-paper method and the invisible machine-appliqué technique found in designer Kim Diehl's books. For free, downloadable information on appliqué techniques, visit ShopMartingale.com/HowtoQuilt.

2 Using straight, not diagonal, seams, join the green bias strips to make four strips, 24" long. Press the seam allowances to one side, all in the same direction.

3 Fold a 24"-long strip lengthwise, wrong sides together, and sew the long raw edges to make a tube. Press the tube flat, centering the seam allowances so they are not visible from the front of the stem. Apply small dots of liquid fabric glue every ½" under the seam allowances and use a hot, dry iron to heat set the seam allowances in place. Make four.

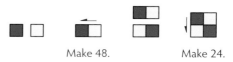

TUBE TIPS

Bias tubes made for appliqué are sewn with wrong sides together, so no turning is required. You can use a ½" bias pressing bar, if desired, to assist in accurately pressing the tube flat.

Making Block A

Stitch all pieces with right sides together and a ¼" seam allowance unless otherwise noted.

1 Draw a line from corner to corner on the wrong side of each assorted-print 3½" square. Place a marked square on one corner of a medium-light neutral 10½" square, right sides together, and sew on the drawn line. Trim the excess corner fabric ¼" from the sewn line and press the triangle toward the corner.

2 Repeat step 1 to attach a second marked square to the opposite corner of the 10½" square. Make 13.

Make 13.

Making Block B

1 Sew an assorted-print 3" square to a light-neutral 3" square to make a two-patch unit. Press the seam allowances toward the darker square. Make 48.

2 Sew the two-patch units together in pairs to make four-patch units. Press the seam allowances to one side. Make 24.

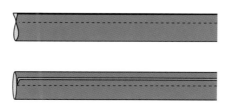

Make 48.   Make 24.

3 Arrange two four-patch units and two assorted-print 5½" squares as shown, noting the orientation of each four-patch unit. Sew the units in each row together, pressing the seam allowances toward the 5½" square. Join the rows to make block B. Press the seam allowances to one side. Make 12.

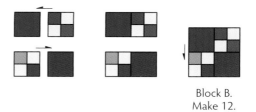

Block B.
Make 12.

Assembling the Quilt

1 Lay out the A and B blocks in an alternating arrangement, orienting the blocks as shown.

2 Sew the blocks together in rows. Press the seam allowances toward the A blocks.

3 Join the rows to make the quilt top and press the seam allowances in one direction.

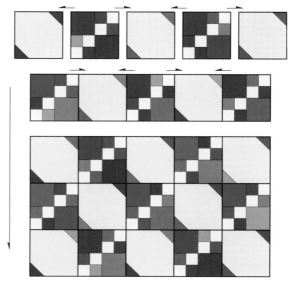

Quilt assembly

Adding the Borders

1 Sew an assorted-print 5⅞" triangle to a dark-neutral 5⅞" triangle along the long bias edge, being careful not to stretch the fabric. Press the seam allowances toward the assorted-print triangle. Trim away the dog-ear corners to square up the unit. Make 20.

Make 20.

2 Divide the half-square-triangle units into two groups, with one unit of each assorted print in each group. Sew 10 half-square-triangle units together, orienting the units as shown, to make a top border. Press the seam allowances in one direction. Make a second border, rotating the units as shown, for the bottom of the quilt.

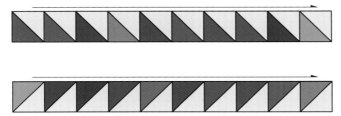

Make 1 of each .

3 Sew the borders to the top and bottom of the quilt.

Appliquéing the Quilt

1 Referring to the quilt photo on page 46 for placement, arrange the appliqués on the quilt top as shown.

2 Working in layers from the bottom to the top, glue baste the stems to the quilt top, and then pin or thread baste the remaining appliqués, ensuring that any raw fabric edges are overlapped by at least ¼". Stitch the appliqués in place.

Finishing the Quilt

1 Cut and piece the backing fabric so it measures at least 56" x 66". Layer the quilt top, batting, and backing. Baste the layers together. Hand or machine quilt as desired. The quilt shown was machine quilted with small swirled circles filling the areas behind the appliqués and the patchwork blocks, with the appliqué designs shadow quilted in the open areas. The borders were quilted with straight lines to echo the triangles.

2 Trim the backing and batting even with the quilt top.

3 Bind the quilt using the dark-blue 2½"-wide strips. Add a hanging sleeve, if desired, and a label.

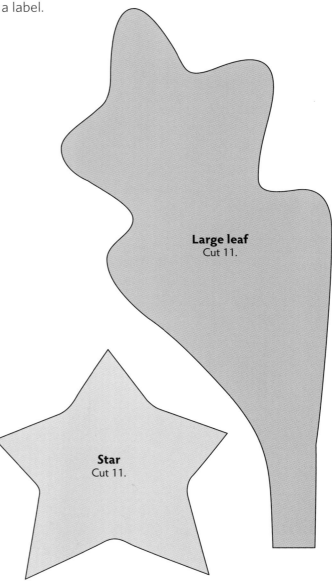

Large leaf
Cut 11.

Star
Cut 11.

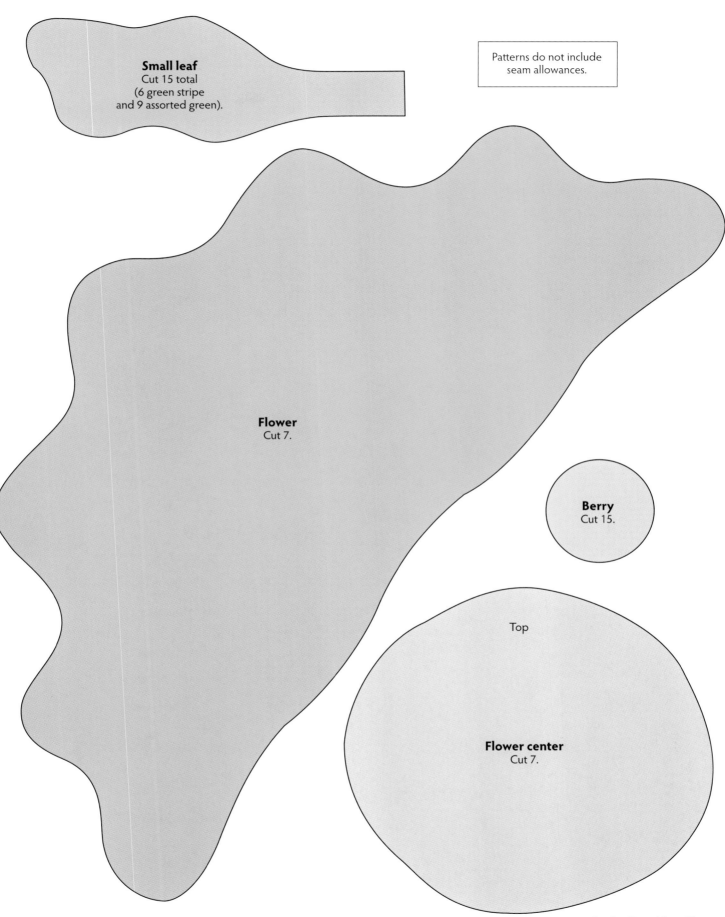

Small leaf
Cut 15 total
(6 green stripe
and 9 assorted green).

Patterns do not include
seam allowances.

Flower
Cut 7.

Berry
Cut 15.

Top

Flower center
Cut 7.

Changing the Meaning of Colors

Pop quiz: **What do the colors red and green** remind you of? Chances are the the first thing that comes to mind are thoughts of Christmas or the holiday season. But red and green abound year 'round in many ways. Think of these red/green combinations in summer: red geraniums against leafy green foliage or a bright red barn against a pasture of green grass.

Designer Kim Diehl often showcases a rich autumnal palette that incorporates red and green too, such as in the collection at right.

But when you've got leftover fabrics from a first project that fall into the "I know I can make something seasonal with this, but what else can I do?" category, how do you jump-start a new mix? Read on.

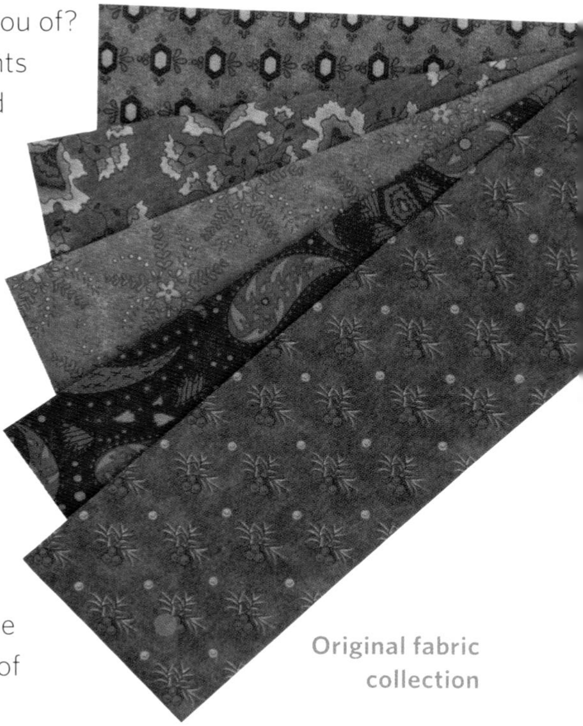

Deconstructing the Details

If what you loved about the original collection was its seasonal feeling, then consider using the remaining prints (shown below at the bottom of the assortment) to spin a new seasonal palette, knowing of course that you have options beyond the expected Christmas route.

Original fabric collection

A medium-scale flower print on a light neutral background is the ideal print to segue this assortment into spring. The simple flower motif is in keeping with the mood of the first two prints and shares a hint of green and a splash of red to hold the continuity among colors. A pair of batiks in the same colors but different shades of green and yellow round out the mix. The new green batik has a springtime, new-leaf hue that draws the palette away from the holiday look.

Another key factor in creating a secondary palette from your stash is this: not balancing the colors in equal proportion often results in a more interesting mix. In this palette, we added more green but not more red to skew the mix toward a springlike feel.

Secondary fabric assortment

Posy Pot Heat Bag

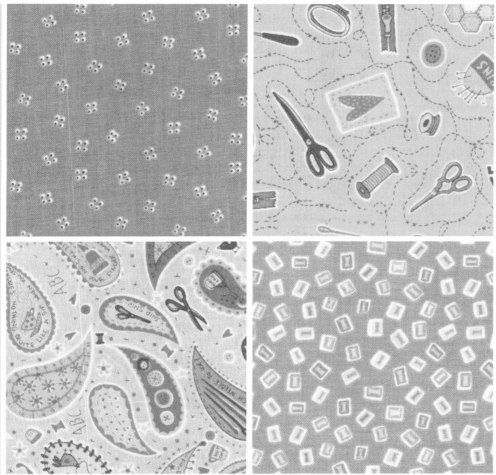

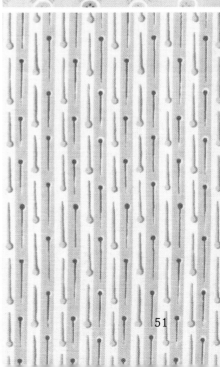

MEET ANNI DOWNS

I love to garden and that passion fuels the earthy tones and muddy colors that I choose for my fabric designs. I'm most comfortable with a blend of fabrics that doesn't scream at me, so I lean toward a muted palette without too much contrast.

It's a personal preference, really, how much contrast you enjoy. Use what makes you happy.

I always include a bit of blue in my collections. It's my favorite color and I find it's a real "popper." —Anni Downs

Posy Pot Heat Bag
Designed and pieced by Anni Downs
of Hatched and Patched
Finished heat-bag size: 6" x 15"

Materials

Yardage is based on 42"-wide fabric, except where noted. Fat eighths measure 9" x 21".

1 fat quarter of muslin for inner bag
1 fat eighth of cream print for background
1 fat eighth of brown floral for lining
1 fat eighth of fabric for backing
Scraps of assorted medium-to-dark prints for checkerboard front
Scraps of assorted light-to-medium prints for appliqué
Embroidery floss in green, blue, yellow, and dark brown
45" of dark gray chenille trim
Three ¾"-diameter buttons
Freezer paper
3 to 4 cups of wheat, barley, buckwheat husks, or uncooked long-grain rice for filling

AROMA THERAPY

For a fragrant heat bag, add 3 tablespoons of dried lavender or other herbs, cloves, or cinnamon for fragrance. Substitute a few drops of an essential oil, if desired.

Cutting

From the medium-to-dark prints, cut:
18 squares, 1½" x 1½"

From the brown floral, cut:
1 rectangle, 4" x 6½"

From the fabric for backing, cut:
1 rectangle, 6½" x 15½"

From the muslin, cut:
2 rectangles, 6½" x 15½"

Appliquéing the Heat Bag

Using a removable marking tool, trace the cutting line of the appliqué rectangle onto the background fabric, leaving at least ½" on all four sides for fabric distortions and fraying while stitching. Don't cut the exact appliqué-panel size until you have completed all the stitching.

This project has been made using needle-turn appliqué for a traditional look. Create a template for each flower shape by tracing the patterns on pages 54 and 55 onto freezer paper. Add areas for overlap as indicated by the dashed lines. Cut out each template on the drawn lines.

Press each template onto the right side of the corresponding fabric with a warm iron, leaving ½" between templates. Cut out the shapes, adding seam allowance as you cut. Pin the shapes to the background as shown in the photo on page 52. Appliqué each shape by hand, turning under the seam allowance as you work. Remove the freezer paper from the appliqués.

If you choose to use fusible appliqué, reverse each appliqué pattern as you trace it. Visit ShopMartingale.com/HowtoQuilt for free, downloadable instructions for a variety of appliqué techniques.

Making the Outer Bag

Stitch all pieces with right sides together and a ¼" seam allowance unless otherwise noted.

1 Working on the appliquéd panel, backstitch the stems by hand, using three strands of green floss. Backstitch the bees with three strands of floss, using dark-brown floss for the bodies (including the stripes) and blue floss for the wings. Use three strands of yellow floss to add a stitch or two between the body stripes.

3 1 2

Backstitch

2 When the stitching is complete, trim the appliquéd fabric to measure 6½" x 14" as shown in the pattern. The margin on the left side is larger than the others, and should measure 2¼" wide.

3 Lay out the 18 medium-to-dark 1½" squares in six columns of three squares each. Press the seam allowances in alternating directions from column to column. Sew the squares in each column together, and then join the columns to make an 18-patch unit measuring 3½" x 6½". Press the seam allowances in one direction.

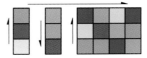

4 Place the brown-floral rectangle on the pieced unit, right sides together, matching one long edge. Sew along the matched long edge and press the seam allowances away from the pieced unit. Turn the brown-floral rectangle to the wrong side, matching the three raw edges; ¼" of the brown rectangle will remain visible on the right side where it wraps around the seam allowances. Press the assembled unit flat.

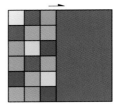 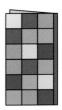

5 Turn ½" to the wrong side along the left edge of the appliquéd rectangle and press. Turn another ½" to the wrong side and press to make a double hem. Topstitch the hem in place.

6 With right sides up, place the pieced unit on the appliquéd rectangle, overlapping the hemmed edges by 1". Adjust the placement as necessary so that the entire front measures 6½" x 15½". Baste the top and bottom edges along the overlap to secure.

7 Pin the 6½" x 15½" backing rectangle to the assembled front, right sides together, and sew around all four sides. Finish the seams using a zigzag or overcast stitch.

8 Turn the heat bag right side out through the overlapped opening. Sew three buttons to the edge of the pieced flap, stitching through the flap only. Hand stitch the chenille trim along the outside seam line of the heat bag with matching thread.

Making the Inner Bag

1 Sew the two muslin rectangles together around all four sides, leaving an opening in one short edge for turning and filling. Turn the bag right side out.

2 Fill the bag about two-thirds full with grain. Add herbs or essential oil to the grain to make the bag particularly aromatic and soothing to use.

3 Turn the seam allowances to the wrong side and sew the opening closed.

4 Insert the grain-filled bag into the cover through the opening beneath the buttons.

USING YOUR HEAT BAG

To use, heat the bag in a microwave oven for about two to three minutes (depending on the strength of the microwave). Place a small glass of water into the microwave to prevent the grain from drying out.

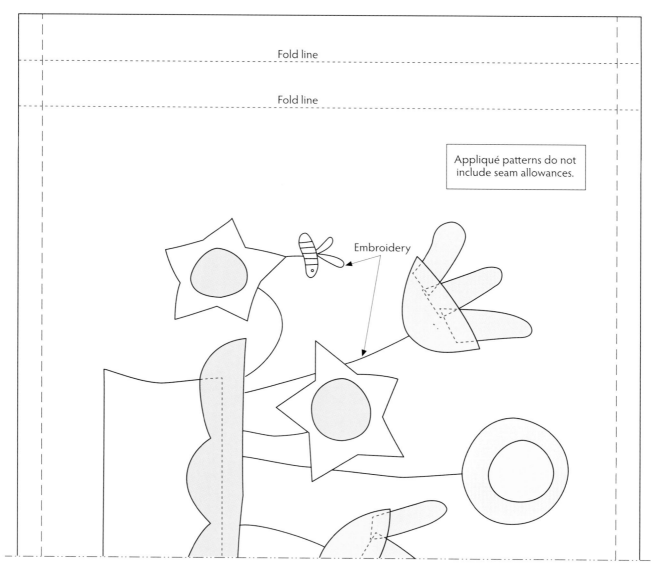

Fold line

Fold line

Appliqué patterns do not include seam allowances.

Embroidery

Join to pattern on page 55.

Join to pattern on page 54.

¼" seam allowance

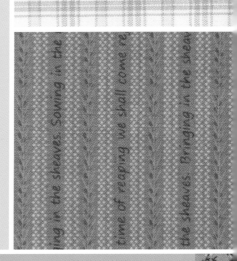

MEET JANET NESBITT AND PAM SOLIDAY

"The must-have in our collections would be a plaid—or three! We use plaids like other quilters use florals. (It's not that we don't like flowers, but when they appear in our prints they need to be able to stay in their color group.) We also always try to include some sort of stripe, either printed or woven, and a word print.

One quilt-shop gal once joked that we are "women of darkness" because our quilts always have a good rich red, paired with a strong gold, and even a black. However, we also love the fall palette that adds in pumpkin, plum, and green. It's important to have a mix of different scales in each line, but for us, it's really all about color. As designers, narrowing the assortment to three colorways per design is tough—so please know you're looking at the cream of our crop every time!"

Don't Forget the Basics

At Buggy Barn, we're quilters, just like you. And at our shop, one of the most common complaints from quilters wanting to create from a single fabric collection is that there are never enough light background choices. Over the years, as we pared down collections to a manageable assortment, the need to keep a meaningful number of background fabrics in the line sometimes presented a challenge. But knowing how important those basics are to creating a quilt, we didn't abandon the cause! Instead, we created Creamery Neutrals, Buggy Barn Basics, and BB Yarn-Dye Basics— collections that are all about basic background fabrics.

Now we have lots to choose from, add to, and mix into a new line or our next quilts!

I love scrap quilts. If I could, my fabric lines would be HUGE and no one would ask me to pare them down to a reasonable selection. That's the difference between being a fabric designer and selecting an assortment of fabrics for myself.

—Designer Janet Nesbitt

Starburst Maple Delight
Designed by Janet Nesbitt and Pam Soliday of Buggy Barn; pieced and quilted by Kathleen Woods
Finished quilt size: 76½" x 96½"
Finished block size: 20" x 20"

Materials

Yardage is based on 42"-wide fabric.

½ yard *each* of 7 assorted red prints for blocks
½ yard *each* of 4 assorted orange prints for blocks
½ yard *each* of 5 assorted green prints for blocks
⅜ yard *each* of 4 assorted cream prints for blocks
⅜ yard *each* of 6 assorted brown prints for blocks
⅞ yard of red plaid for inner border
1½ yards of brown print for outer border
⅝ yard of fabric for binding
5¾ yards of fabric for backing
82" x 102" piece of batting

Cutting

Cutting instructions are for one block; cut 12. For each of the 12 blocks, select one red print (red #1) for the center star and one green print for the star background, plus one each of the cream, orange, and brown prints, plus a second red print (red #2).

Cutting for One Block

From red print #1, cut:
1 square, 5½" x 5½"
8 squares, 3" x 3"

From red print #2, cut:
4 squares, 3⅜" x 3⅜"
4 squares, 3" x 3"

From the green print, cut:
8 rectangles, 3" x 5½"
4 squares, 3" x 3"

From the brown print, cut:
4 squares, 3⅜" x 3⅜"
16 squares, 3" x 3"

From the cream print, cut:
4 squares, 3⅜" x 3⅜"
8 squares, 3" x 3"

From the orange print, cut:
4 rectangles, 3" x 5½"
4 squares, 3⅜" x 3⅜"
4 squares, 3" x 3"

Cutting for Borders and Binding

From the red plaid, cut:
8 strips, 3½" x 42"

From the brown print, cut:
9 strips, 5½" x 42"

From the fabric for binding, cut:
9 strips, 2¼" x 42"

Making the Blocks

Stitch all pieces with right sides together and a ¼" seam allowance unless otherwise noted. Instructions are for making one block at a time. Make 12 blocks total.

1 Draw a diagonal line from corner to corner on the wrong side of each 3" red #1 square. Place a marked square on the left end of a green 3" x 5½" rectangle, right sides together, and sew on the drawn line. Trim the excess corner fabric ¼" from the sewn line and press the seam allowances toward the corner.

2 Repeat step 1 to sew a second marked square on the right end of the rectangle to complete a flying-geese unit. Make four.

3 Make eight more flying-geese units, four with the cream 3" squares and green rectangles and four with the brown 3" squares and orange 3" x 5½" rectangles.

Make 4.   Make 4.   Make 4.

4 Draw a diagonal line from corner to corner on the wrong side of each cream 3⅜" square. Place a marked square on an orange 3⅜" square, right sides together, and sew ¼" from each side of the drawn line. Cut on the drawn line and press the seam allowances toward the orange triangles to make two half-square-triangle units. Make eight.

5 Repeat step 4 with the red and brown 3⅜" squares to make eight more half-square-triangle units, pressing the seam allowances toward the brown triangles.

Make 8.   Make 8.

6 Arrange the flying-geese and half-square-triangle units with the red 5½" square and the 3" green, orange, brown, and red #2 squares in seven rows of seven units each, orienting each unit as shown on page 60.

7 Sew the units together in rows, pressing the seam allowances in alternating directions from row to row.

8 Join the rows to complete a block. Press the seam allowances in one direction. Make 12 blocks.

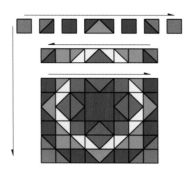

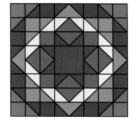

Make 12.

Assembling the Quilt

1 Lay out the blocks in four rows of three blocks each. Rotate the blocks so adjacent seam allowances lie in opposite directions for easier piecing.

2 Sew the blocks together in rows. Press the seam allowances in alternating directions from row to row. Join the rows to complete the quilt top, pressing the seam allowances in one direction.

Adding the Borders

1 Sew the red-plaid strips together end to end to make a long strip. Crosscut the long strip into two strips, 80½" long, and two strips, 66½" long.

2 Sew the 80½"-long strips to the sides of the quilt. Press the seam allowances toward the inner border. Sew the 66½"-long strips to the top and bottom of the quilt. Press the seam allowances toward the inner border.

3 Sew the brown-print strips together end to end to make a long strip. Crosscut the long strip into two strips, 86½" long, and two strips, 76½" long.

4 Sew the 86½"-long strips to the sides of the quilt. Press the seam allowances toward the outer border. Sew the 76½"-long strips to the top and bottom of the quilt. Press the seam allowances toward the outer border.

Quilt assembly

Finishing the Quilt

1 Cut and piece the backing fabric so it measures about 82" x 102".

2 Layer the quilt top, batting, and backing. Baste the layers together. Hand or machine quilt as desired. The quilt shown was machine quilted with large, pointed flowers in the star blocks, a loop-de-loop pattern in the inner border, and feathers in the outer border.

3 Trim the backing and batting even with the quilt top.

4 Bind the quilt using the 2¼"-wide binding strips. Add a hanging sleeve, if desired, and a label.

Peaceful Patchwork Rich with Texture

Having a lively assortment of prints to begin a project with appeals to the aesthetic of many quilters. And when those prints are a predetermined mix of fabrics, such as Buggy Barn's collection at right, it makes choosing and combining fabrics for a project easy. The designers intend for this collection of prints to work together in a quilt—and they do. But after the project is complete, is it possible to soften the mix of prints when pulling together a secondary palette with your leftovers, while still keeping it interesting? Indeed, it is!

Deconstructing the Details

A monochromatic or low-contrast quilt can result in a sophisticated look, but choosing fabrics with some richness in their textures is essential. For example, the two remaining neutral prints at the top of the photo at right provided the starting point for the restful secondary palette below.

The grouping is expanded in both light and dark directions with the addition of three new tone-on-tone prints. The darkest brown print has a linen-like texture overprinted on the cloth, adding depth to the overall look. The two lighter prints also repeat the textured background appearance, as well as bringing in two medium-scale designs for balance against the other small-scale prints.

The one original tan fabric at the bottom of the stack has more yellow than the others in the mix, but using it sparingly in a design will help give a quilt top some sparkle without adding an altogether different color to the monochromatic palette.

Original fabric collection

Secondary fabric assortment

Line upon Line

MEET AMY HAMBERLIN

"*With any kind of creative venture,* we each discover things about ourselves we didn't know, which is what I love about quilting. The process of picking a project, auditioning fabrics, and a healthy dose of sewing is exciting and creative. Fabric design plays a leading role in our individual creative processes too. It becomes part of who we are, and I love it!"

I know a fabric line is ready when I love each piece individually, two by two, and most importantly, all together. Try that same test when you're culling fabrics for a project, keeping your mind open to changes as things start to take shape. —Amy Hamberlin

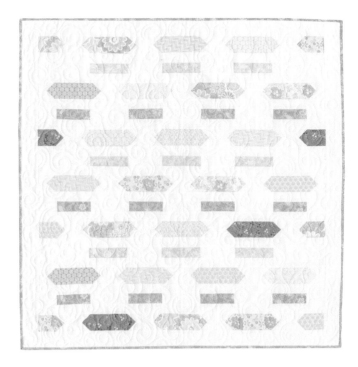

Line upon Line
Designed, pieced, and quilted by
Amy Hamberlin of Kati Cupcake Pattern Co.

Finished quilt size: 38½" x 41"

Materials

Yardage is based on 42"-wide fabric, except where noted. Fat eighths measure 9" x 21".

1 fat eighth *each* of 12 coordinating prints for blocks
1 fat eighth of blue tone on tone for sashing
1¾ yards of white solid for background
⅝ yard of pink tone on tone for sashing and binding
2½ yards of fabric for backing*
44" x 46" piece of batting

*If your fabric is wide enough, you may purchase just 1⅓ yards of fabric and use a single length for the backing.

Cutting

From the white solid, cut:
112 squares, 2½" x 2½"
6 rectangles, 1¾" x 2¾"
6 rectangles, 1¾" x 4½"
9 rectangles, 1¾" x 5"
6 rectangles, 1¾" x 6¾"
12 strips, 1¾" x 34½"
2 strips, 2½" x 34½"
2 strips, 2½" x 40½"

From the coordinating prints, cut:
24 rectangles, 2½" x 9"
8 rectangles, 2½" x 4¾"

From the pink tone on tone, cut:
12 rectangles, 1¾" x 4½"
5 strips, 2½" x 42"

From the blue tone on tone, cut:
9 rectangles, 1¾" x 5"

Making the Blocks and Units

Stitch all pieces with right sides together and a ¼" seam allowance unless otherwise noted.

1 Draw a line from corner to corner on the wrong side of each white square. With right sides together, place a marked square on each end of a print 2½" x 9" rectangle, orienting the drawn lines as shown. Sew on the lines. Trim the excess corner fabric ¼" from each sewn line and press the seam allowances toward the corners.

2 Place another marked square on each end of the rectangle, orienting the drawn lines in the opposite direction. Sew on the lines. Trim the excess corner fabric ¼" from each sewn line and press the seam allowances toward the corners. Make 24 blocks.

Make 24.

3 With right sides together, place a marked square on the left end of a print 2½" x 4¾" rectangle, orienting the drawn line as shown. Sew on the line. Trim and press as before.

4 Place a second marked square on the left end of the same rectangle, positioning the line in the opposite direction. Sew on the line. Trim and press as before. Make four A units in assorted print colors.

Unit A.
Make 4.

5 Repeat steps 3 and 4, placing the marked squares on the right end of a print 2½" x 4¾" rectangle and orienting the lines as shown. Make four B units.

Unit B.
Make 4.

Making the Block Rows

1 Sew four assorted blocks together, rotating every other one 180°, to make row 1. Press the seam allowances open. Make three.

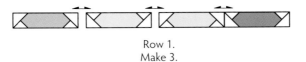

Row 1.
Make 3.

2 Sew three assorted blocks together, rotating every other one 180°. Sew A and B units to each end of the row as shown to make row 2. Press the seam allowances open. Make four.

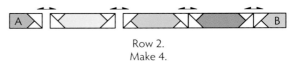

Row 2.
Make 4.

TURN FOR THE BETTER

While the block rotation will be nearly invisible in the finished quilt, it distributes seam allowance bulk for a neater result . . . and fewer seams to match.

Making the Sashing Strips

1 Sew three white 1¾" x 5" rectangles and four pink tone-on-tone rectangles together end to end, alternating the colors as shown. Add a white 1¾" x 2¾" rectangle to each end of the pieced strip. Press the seam allowances toward the pink rectangles.

2 Sew white 1¾" x 34½" strips to the top and bottom of the pieced unit to make a pink sashing strip. Press the seam allowances toward the white strips. Make three.

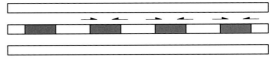

Make 3.

3 Sew two white 1¾" x 4½" rectangles and three blue tone-on-tone rectangles together end to end, alternating the colors as shown. Add a white 1¾" x 6¾" rectangle to each end of the pieced unit.

4 Sew white 1¾" x 34½" strips to the top and bottom of the pieced unit to make a blue sashing strip. Make three.

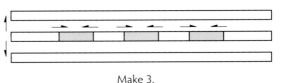

Make 3.

Assembling the Quilt

1 Arrange the seven block rows and six sashing strips as shown in the assembly diagram below.

2 Sew the rows together to complete the quilt top. Press the seam allowances in one direction.

Adding the Border

1 Sew the white 34½"-long strips to the top and bottom of the quilt. Press the seam allowances toward the border.

2 Sew the white 40½"-long strips to the sides of the quilt. Press the seam allowances toward the border.

Finishing the Quilt

1 Cut and piece the backing fabric so it is 6" longer and wider than the quilt top.

2 Layer the quilt top, batting, and backing. Baste the layers together. Hand or machine quilt as desired. The quilt shown was machine quilted with an allover swirl design.

3 Trim the backing and batting even with the quilt top.

4 Bind the quilt using the pink 2½"-wide strips. Add a hanging sleeve, if desired, and a label.

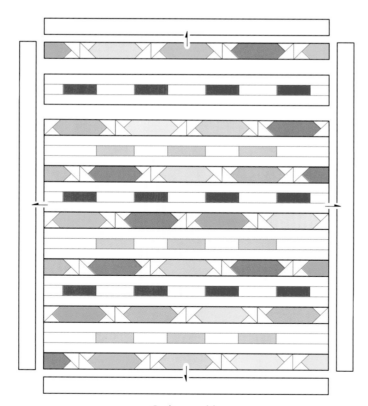

Quilt assembly

Caboodle
Quilting Caddy

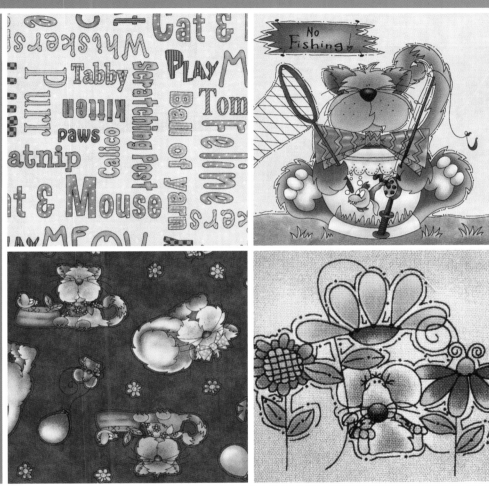

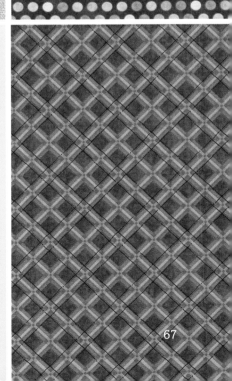

MEET LEANNE ANDERSON

" *I am a woman of faith,* and each of my collections reflects the blessings in my life. Whether it is the creation story in my "In the Beginning" group or the story of what a gift a child is in my collection "God Gave Me You," I want the fabrics I design to speak to quilters and cultivate in them a desire to create—not only because of what the fabrics look like, but for what they say and represent. "

Caboodle Quilting Caddy
Designed and pieced by
Leanne Anderson of The Whole Country Caboodle

Finished case size: 14" x 32" open, 14" x 14½" closed

Designing fabric is an answer to a prayer. It has given me the opportunity to share my faith through what I design. That is a wonderful gift!

—Leanne Anderson

Materials

Yardage is based on 42"-wide fabric.

1⅛ yards of green swirl print for body, outside pockets, and handle

⅞ yard of green houndstooth for lining, binding, and closures

½ yard of green star print for inside pockets and tab closures

15" x 33" piece of batting

1¼ yards of ¼"-wide elastic

14" zipper

Two 1½" D rings

Two 1½" swivel hooks

Two 1"-diameter buttons

Seven ⅝"-diameter buttons

Cutting

From the green swirl print, cut:

1 rectangle, 15" x 33"

1 rectangle, 14" x 17"

1 rectangle, 14" x 25"

1 strip, 5½" x 42"

From the green houndstooth, cut:

1 rectangle, 15" x 33"

3 strips, 2¼" x 42"

1 strip, 4" x 42"

From the green star print, cut:

1 rectangle, 6½" x 15"

1 rectangle, 3½" x 9"

1 rectangle, 5½" x 13"

1 strip, 3" x 18"

1 rectangle, 12" x 14"

1 rectangle, 7½" x 8"

1 rectangle, 4" x 9"

1 rectangle, 3" x 7½"

Quilting the Body

1 Create a quilt sandwich from the 15" x 33" houndstooth, batting, and swirl-print rectangles. Baste the layers together.

2 Machine quilt the pieces as desired. Trim the quilted fabric to measure 14" x 32" for the body of the caddy.

Adding the Inside Pockets

Stitch all pieces with right sides together and a ¼" seam allowance unless otherwise noted. As you follow these instructions, picture the caddy body in a horizontal orientation, with its long edges at top and bottom.

1 Fold the star-print 6½" x 15", 3½" x 9", and 5½" x 13" rectangles in half, wrong sides together, and press to make pockets measuring 6½" x 7½", 3½" x 4½", and 5½" x 6½". The folded edges become the tops of the pockets.

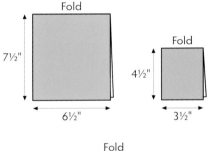
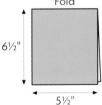

2 On the houndstooth side of the quilted body, measure 9½" from the short right end and draw a line from top to bottom.

3 Position the pockets on the body as shown, folding ½" to the wrong side along the inner edges of the larger pockets. The pockets' bottom edges should lie along the line from step 2. The side edges of the smallest pocket overlap the other pockets by ¼".

4 Stitch ¼" to the left of the marked line, ¼" from the bottom of the pockets. Press the pockets to the right, covering the seam allowances, and pin in place. Edgestitch the larger pockets along their side folds and again ¼" inside the folds, backstitching to reinforce the stitches and catching the raw edges of the smallest pocket.

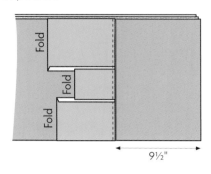

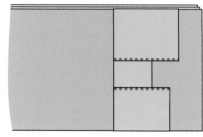

5 Fold the star-print 3" x 18" strip in half lengthwise, wrong sides together, and press. Open the strip and fold the raw edges to meet at the center crease line. Press again. Refold the strip along the original crease, enclosing the raw edges, and press again to make the closure strip. Edgestitch both long edges and topstitch down the center of the strip. Crosscut the strip into three closure-tab pieces, 4" long.

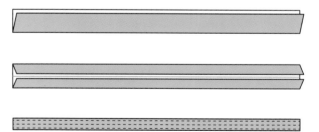

6 Press ¼" to the wrong side on one end of each closure tab and topstitch to create a hem. Stitch a buttonhole for a ⅝"-diameter button along the centerline and ⅜" from the hemmed end of each piece.

7 Slip ½" of the unfinished end of a closure tab, wrong side up, under the center of each pocket. Machine stitch ¼" from the raw edge of the closure tab through the tab and body to securely attach each closure tab to the body.

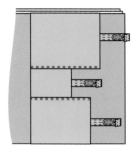

8 Fold the star-print 12" x 14" rectangle in half, wrong sides together, and press to make a pocket measuring 6" x 14". Measure 11" from the right end of the body interior and draw a line from top to bottom. Align the raw edges of the pocket with the marked line as shown.

9 Stitch ¼" to the right of the marked line, ¼" from the bottom of the pocket. Press the pocket to the left, covering the seam allowances, and pin in place.

10 Measure 1⅜" from the top and draw a line across the pocket. Draw four more lines, 1" apart, below the first. Sew on the lines, creating five pencil pockets.

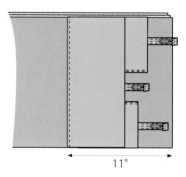

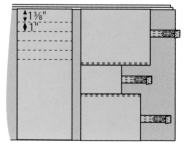

11 Fold the star-print 7½" x 8" rectangle into thirds to measure 2½" x 8" and press. Bind the three raw edges of the flap (the long edge with a raw edge visible and both short ends) with a houndstooth 2¼" x 42" strip; reserve the leftover strip for later use. Stitch two buttonholes for ⅝"-diameter buttons, each ¾" from the side of the flap and ½" above its long bound edge.

12 Slip ½" of the unbound flap edge under the pocket, aligning the edge of the flap with the centermost pencil-pocket stitching. Position the flap wrong side up. Stitch ¼" from the unbound edge of the flap, through the flap and body only, to attach it to the body. Press the flap to the right, over the pocket edge.

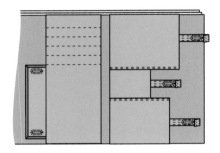

13 Fold the star-print 4" x 9" rectangle in half, wrong sides together, and press to make a pocket measuring 4" x 4½". With the folded edge at the top, press ½" to the wrong side along the left edge of the pocket.

14 Measure 1" from the top of the pencil pockets and draw a 3½"-long line parallel to the pencil-pocket openings. Align the raw bottom edge of the new pocket with the marked line as shown. Stitch ¼" to the right of the marked line, ¼" from the bottom of the pocket. Press the pocket to the left and pin in place. Edgestitch the pocket along the side fold and topstitch ¼" from the same fold.

15 Fold the star-print 3" x 7½" rectangle into thirds to measure 2½" x 3" and press. Bind the three raw edges with the remainder of the houndstooth strip from step 11. Stitch two buttonholes for ⅝"-diameter buttons, each ¾" from the side of the flap and ½" above its lower edge.

16 Slip ½" of the unbound flap edge under the pocket, aligning the edge of the flap with the topstitching. Sew the flap edge to the body of the caddy by stitching ¼" above the flap's unbound edge, through the flap and body only. Press the flap to the right, over the pocket edge.

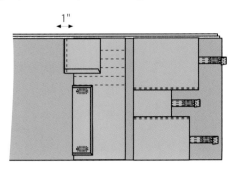

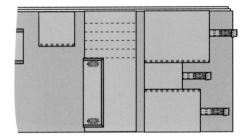

Adding the Elastic Holders

1 Cut the ¼"-wide elastic into two 2½" lengths and two 18" lengths. Mark ¼" from the ends of each elastic length. In addition, make marks 3½" apart to divide the 17½" center area of each longer piece into five equal sections.

2 Measure 1¾" from the top of the wide flap pocket and draw a line parallel to the pocket with a removable marking tool. Make cross marks 2", 3⅝", 5¼", 6⅞", and 8½" from the bottom edge of the body. Lay one 18" elastic length along the line, matching the first line on the elastic to the seamline on the body; baste the elastic to the body just inside the seam allowance. Match the next line on the elastic to the 2" cross mark and sew back and forth across the elastic to secure it to the caddy. Repeat to match and stitch the remaining marks. The elastic will bow upward, making loops to hold spools of thread.

3 Measure 2½" to the left of the first elastic band and repeat the marking and stitching processes to make five more spool loops.

4 Sew the 2½" elastic lengths to the body of the caddy between the spool loops and the small pocket in the same way, spacing the marks on the body of the caddy along the path of each elastic about 1¼" apart, to hold a measuring tape.

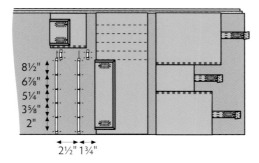

Adding the Outside Pockets

1 Fold the swirl-print 14" x 25" and 14" x 17" rectangles in half, wrong sides together, and press to make pockets measuring 12½" x 14" and 8½" x 14".

2 Rearrange the caddy so the outside of the body is facing up and the first pockets you attached are on the right. Measure 10½" from the right end of the body and draw a line from top to bottom. Align the raw edges of the 12½" x 14" pocket with the marked line as shown.

3 Stitch ¼" to the right of the marked line, ¼" from the bottom of the pocket. This stitching line will fall between the rows of pockets on the inside of the caddy. Press the pocket to the left and pin in place.

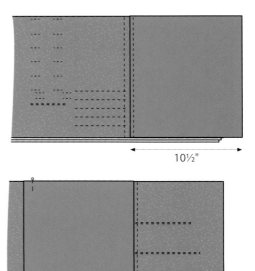

4 Center the folded edge of the remaining pocket on the zipper tape, right side up, ⅛" from the zipper teeth. Using a zipper foot, edgestitch next to the fold. Press ¼" to the wrong side along the edge of the pocket opposite the zipper.

5 Measure 2½" from the right end of the body and draw a line from top to bottom. Place the zippered pocket, wrong side up, on the body with the free edge of the zipper tape along the line, aligning the raw edges of the pocket with the raw edges of the body. Use a zipper foot to stitch the

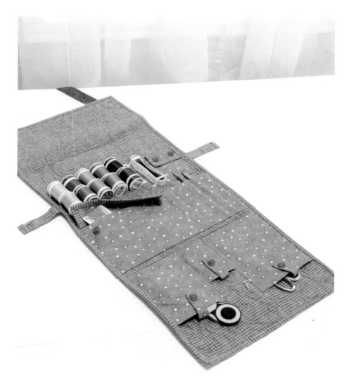

free edge of the zipper to the caddy body. Flip the pocket to the left, turning the zipper right side up, and pin in place. Edgestitch the pocket's pressed edge to the body.

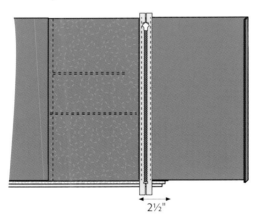

2½"

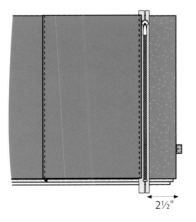

2½"

6 Unzip the zipper half way. Carefully stitch back and forth across the zipper ⅛" from the caddy's raw edges. Trim the zipper tape at each end to match the caddy fabric.

Finishing the Caddy

1 Using the remaining houndstooth 2¼" x 42" strips, bind all four sides of the caddy, beginning in the middle of one side.

2 Fold the houndstooth 4" x 42" strip in half lengthwise, wrong sides together, and press. Open the strip and fold the raw edges to meet at the center crease line. Press again. Refold the strip along the original crease, enclosing the raw edges, and press once more. Edgestitch both long edges and topstitch along the center of the strip. Crosscut the closure strip into two tabs, 5" long, and two D-ring loops, 2½" long.

3 Press ½" to the wrong side on one end of each tab and topstitch along the edge and ¼" from the first stitching line. Make a buttonhole for a 1"-diameter button along the centerline, ¾" from the hemmed end of each tab.

4 Press ¼" to the wrong side on the unfinished end of each tab. Pin a tab, right side up, 2½" to the right of the cutting-mat pocket on each side as shown, matching the folded end of the tab with the inner edge of the binding. Topstitch through the tab along the inner and outer edges of the binding.

5 Repeat the pressing from step 2 with the swirl-print 5½" x 42" strip to make the shoulder strap. Edgestitch both long edges and stitch again ¼" from the first stitching line; do not stitch along the centerline. Fold ½" to the wrong side on each end and press.

6 Thread each of the shoulder-strap ends through a 1½" swivel hook, folding an additional 1" to the wrong side. Topstitch next to the pressed edge from step 5 and again ¼" from the first stitching line.

7 Fold ¼" to the wrong side of one end of a D-ring loop from step 2 and press well. Thread the unfolded end through a 1½" D-ring and tuck the raw edge inside the pressed ¼", folding the loop around the D-ring. Make two.

8 Pin the folded and tucked end of a D-ring loop 1¾" to the left of the cutting-mat pocket on each side as shown, positioning the loop along the inner edge of the binding. Topstitch along the pressed end of the loop and ¼" away from the first stitching to secure both ends of the loop.

9 Mark and stitch two buttonholes for 1"-diameter buttons on the end of the caddy without pockets. Each buttonhole should be 1¼" from the long edge and ⅝" from the short edge of the caddy.

10 Fold the caddy closed between the two outside pockets. Fold 6½" down for the flap. Bring the tabs to the front and mark the button locations on the end of the caddy near the zipper; the buttons should be centered between the zipper and the end of the caddy, about 1¼" from the sides of the caddy. Sew a 1"-diameter button at each location.

11 Open the caddy and mark the placements for the ⅝"-diameter buttons. Sew the buttons to the interior pockets. Use the swivel hooks to connect the shoulder strap to the D-rings.

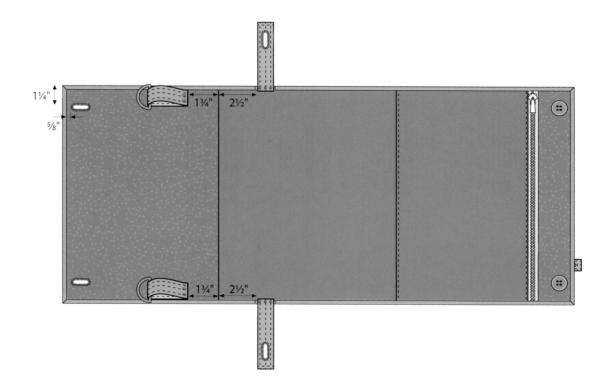

Where Flowers Blossom

MEET LIZ HAWKINS AND BETH HAWKINS

Often the catalyst when we begin designing a collection is music, and usually it's a particular mood! What sings to us about our color palette is that it's gotta be happy! We usually go bold and bright. That's where we're the most comfortable.

We know we've got the right mix for a collection when we can start designing quilts with it in our heads—then we know it's good to go! That same approach works when you're pulling fabrics for a quilt. "

Where Flowers Blossom
Designed and pieced by Liz Hawkins and Beth Hawkins of Lizzie B Cre8ive
Finished quilt size: 18½" x 28½"

Stay true to your color palette! Fabric lines come and go, but as long as you keep the same palette going in a project, it will always come out a winner.

—The Lizzie B Girls

Materials

Yardage is based on 42"-wide fabric, except where noted. Fat quarters measure 18" x 21" and fat eighths measure 9" x 21".

1 fat quarter *each* of blue swirl, cream print, and black swirl for background

1 fat quarter of dark-pink swirl for appliqué

1 fat eighth *each* of 6 assorted green and blue prints for striped panel

Scraps of assorted colors and prints for appliqués and yo-yos

¼ yard of black solid for binding

¾ yard of fabric for backing

24" x 33" piece of batting

Embroidery floss in black and cream

12 buttons in assorted colors and sizes

Cutting

After cutting, reserve the assorted green- and blue-print remnants for appliqués.

From *each* of the 6 assorted green and blue prints, cut:
2 strips in various sizes from ¾"–1¼" wide by 9" long

From the blue swirl, cut:
1 rectangle, 9½" x 18½"

From the cream print, cut:
1 rectangle, 9½" x 18½"

From the black swirl, cut:
1 rectangle, 10½" x 18½"

From the assorted scraps, cut:
3 circles, 5" diameter

From the black solid, cut:
3 strips, 2¼" x 42"

Preparing the Appliqués

Using the patterns on pages 79–86, prepare the appliqués for your chosen method; the sample quilt features needle-turn appliqué with blind-stitch edges. Reverse the patterns if you are using fusible web for the appliqués.

Visit ShopMartingale.com/HowtoQuilt for free, downloadable instructions for a variety of appliqué techniques.

Making the Background

Stitch all pieces with right sides together and a ¼" seam allowance unless otherwise noted.

1 Sew the assorted green and blue strips together in random order to make a striped panel measuring 9" x 12". Cut and attach extra strips or trim the pieced unit as necessary. Press the seam allowances in one direction.

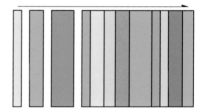

2 Sew the blue-swirl rectangle to the top of the cream-print rectangle. Sew the black-swirl rectangle to the bottom of the cream rectangle. Press the seam allowances open.

3 Measure 9" to the left of the black rectangle's bottom-right corner and make a mark on the raw edge. Measure 5½" above the same corner and make a second mark. Referring to the quilt photo, draw a sloping curve connecting the marks and cut on the drawn line. Press ¼" to the wrong side along the curved edge.

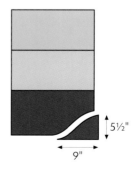

4 Turn the striped panel at a 45° angle and position it under the black rectangle as shown. Edgestitch the black rectangle's pressed edge to the striped panel. Trim the striped panel to align with the bottom and right edges of the black rectangle.

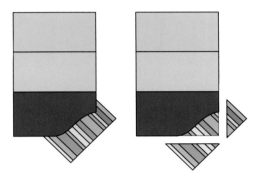

Appliquéing the Quilt

1 Turn ¼" to the wrong side around the edge of each 5" circle. Using two strands of thread, hand sew a basting stitch along the folded edge. Pull the thread to gather the fabric, leaving a small circle open in the center. Make a few backstitches to secure the threads and tie a knot to finish, hiding the knot inside the gathers. Make three yo-yos.

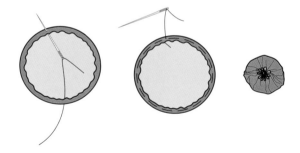

2 Referring to the quilt photo on page 76, place each appliqué shape and letter in position. Using matching thread, appliqué each shape to the quilt top.

3 Trace the words "Where flowers" and "So does" on the blue and black sections of the quilt top. Use black and cream embroidery floss to backstitch the words.

Backstitch

Finishing the Quilt

1 Cut the backing fabric to measure 6" longer and wider than the quilt top. Layer the quilt top, batting, and backing. Baste the layers together.

2 Using cream thread and a running stitch, hand quilt the project, stitching around each appliqué and sewing swirls throughout each open section. Quilt the watering can with a crosshatch design. Trim the backing and batting even with the quilt top.

3 Sew the three yo-yos to the flowers, referring to the quilt photo for placement. Stitch 12 buttons to the yo-yos and flowers as shown.

4 Bind the quilt using the black 2¼"-wide strips. Add a hanging sleeve, if desired, and a label.

Appliqué placement

Align pattern on dashed lines.

Align pattern on dashed lines.

B1

Align pattern on dashed lines.

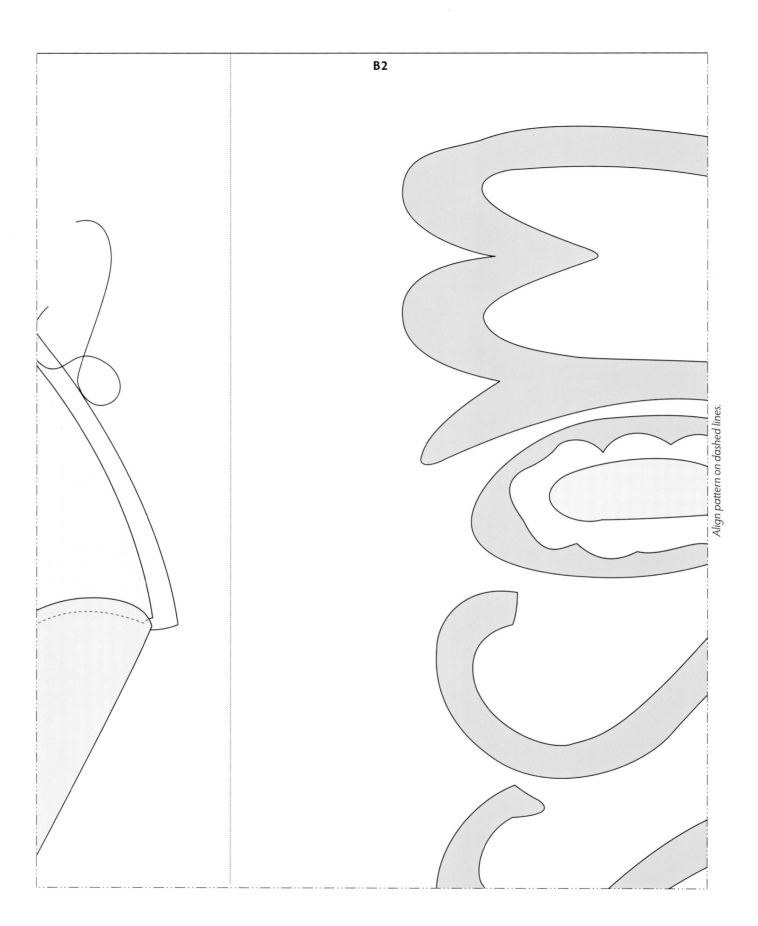

Align pattern on dashed lines.

C1

Align pattern on dashed lines.

Align pattern on dashed lines.

D1

Align pattern on dashed lines.

Align pattern on dashed lines.

Picnic Basket
Table Topper

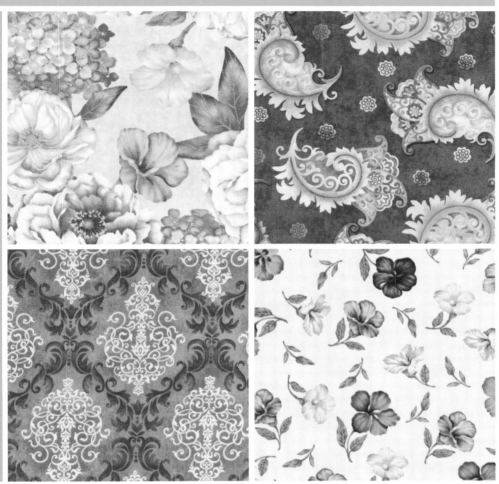

MEET MARGOT LANGUEDOC

" *It was my love of fabric,* my passion for quilting, and teaching at a local quilt shop that started me on the road to designing. My designs have always been about simple and fun patterns that appeal to everyone.

My studio in our country home is built on what was once a Christmas tree farm. It is surrounded with nature's inspiration. "

> *I'm thrilled that I've been able to connect with so many quilters—from young moms making their first quilt to experienced quilters looking for a creative new design.*
>
> —Margot Languedoc

Picnic Basket Table Topper

Designed by Margot Languedoc of
The Pattern Basket

Finished quilt size: 34½" x 34½"

Finished block size: 7½" x 7½"

Materials

Yardage is based on 42"-wide fabric unless otherwise noted. Fat eighths measure 9" x 21".

1¼ yards of light print for blocks, sashing, and border
1 fat eighth *each* of 17 pastel prints for blocks
⅓ yard of pale-pink print for binding
1¼ yards of fabric for backing
40" x 40" piece of batting

Cutting

From the light print, cut:

18 squares, 2⅝" x 2⅝"; cut in half diagonally to yield 36 triangles
2 squares, 2⅛" x 2⅛"
15 strips, 1¾" x 42"; crosscut into:
    54 rectangles, 1¾" x 8"
    18 rectangles, 1¾" x 5½"
    16 squares, 1¾" x 1¾"
2 strips, 2½" x 34½"
2 strips, 2½" x 30½"

From *each* of the assorted pastel prints, cut:

1 square, 2⅝" x 2⅝"; cut in half diagonally to yield 2 triangles. Repeat with 1 of the fabrics to make 36 total.
1 square, 3⅜" x 3⅜"; cut in half diagonally to yield 2 triangles. Repeat with 1 of the fabrics to make 36 total.

From *9* of the assorted pastel prints, cut:

5 squares, 1¾" x 1¾" (45 total)

From *8* of the assorted pastel prints, cut:

4 squares, 1¾" x 1¾" (32 total; 1 will be extra)

From the remainder of the assorted pastel prints, cut a *total* of:

2 squares, 2⅛" x 2⅛"

From the pale-pink print, cut:

4 strips, 2½" x 42"

Making the Blocks

Stitch all pieces with right sides together and a ¼" seam allowance unless otherwise noted. For each block, select a pair of matching print 2⅝" and

3⅜" triangles (print #1), and a coordinating set of matching print triangles (print #2) for the Pinwheel block center. You'll also need four light-print 2⅝" triangles. For the block borders, you'll need four assorted-print 1¾" squares.

These instructions will make one block. Make nine blocks total.

1 Sew a 2⅝" triangle of print #1 to a light-print 2⅝" triangle along one short side, placing print #1 on the bottom as shown. Sew the triangular unit to a 3⅜" triangle of print #2. Make two.

Make 2.

2 Sew a 2⅝" triangle of print #2 to a light-print 2⅝" triangle along one short side, placing print #2 on the bottom as shown. Sew each triangular unit to a 3⅜" triangle of print #1. Make two.

Make 2.

3 Arrange the four units as shown to form a pinwheel. Sew the units together in pairs, pressing the seam allowances in opposite directions. Sew the pairs together to complete a block center measuring 5½" square. Press the seam allowances to one side.

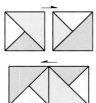

Make 9.

4 Draw a line from corner to corner on the wrong side of an assorted-print 1¾" square. Place the marked square on the left end of a light-print 1¾" x 8" rectangle, orienting the line as shown. Sew on the line. Trim the excess corner fabric ¼" from the sewn line and press the seam allowances toward

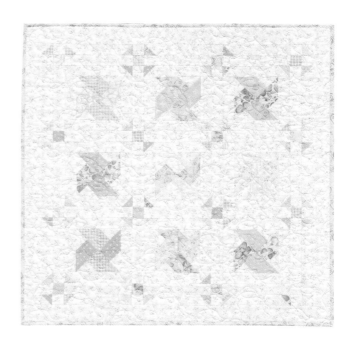

the corner. Repeat on the opposite end of the light rectangle using a different-color print square. Make two.

Make 2.

5 Sew a light-print 1¾" x 5½" rectangle to each side of the pinwheel block center. Sew the units from step 4 to the top and bottom of each unit to make an 8"-square block.

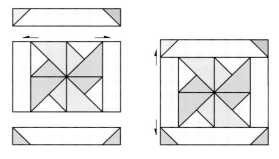

6 Repeat steps 1–5 to make nine blocks. Repeat step 4 to make 12 additional units for use in the borders.

Assembling the Quilt

1 Join four assorted-print 1¾" squares, three light-print 1¾" x 8" rectangles, and two light-print 1¾" squares to make a sashing row. Press the seam allowances to one side. Make four.

Make 4.

2 Arrange the nine blocks as desired, alternating the blocks with light-print 1¾" x 8" rectangles. Add one of the pieced units from the previous section to each end of each row. Be sure the triangles in the border units are oriented as shown. Sew the blocks together in rows, pressing the seam allowances toward the sashing rectangles.

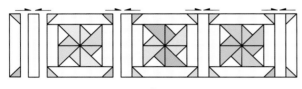

Make 3.

3 Draw a line from corner to corner on the wrong side of each light-print 2⅛" square. Place a light-print square on an assorted-print 2⅛" square, right sides together, and sew ¼" from each side of the drawn line. Cut on the drawn line to make two half-square-triangle units and press, pressing the seam allowances to one side. Trim each unit to measure 1¾" x 1¾". Make four half-square-triangle units.

Make 4.

4 Sew two half-square-triangle units, four light-print 1¾" squares, and three border units together to make the top border, orienting the triangles as shown. Press the seam allowances toward the light-print squares. Repeat to make the bottom border.

Make 2.

5 Sew the sashing rows, block rows, and top and bottom borders together to make the quilt top. Press the seam allowances between rows toward the sashing strips.

6 Sew a light-print 2½" x 30½" strip to each side of the quilt. Sew the light-print 2½" x 34½" strips to the top and bottom of the quilt. Press the seam allowances toward the border.

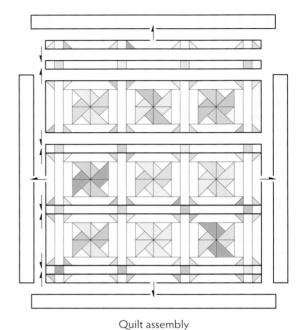

Quilt assembly

Finishing the Quilt

1 Cut the backing fabric 6" longer and wider than the quilt top. Layer the quilt top, batting, and backing. Baste the layers together. Hand or machine quilt as desired. The quilt shown was machine quilted with an allover pattern of swirls and leaves.

2 Trim the backing and batting even with the quilt top, squaring up the quilt sandwich.

3 Bind the quilt using the pale-pink 2½"-wide strips. Add a hanging sleeve, if desired, and a label.

Peppermint Twist Christmas Pillow

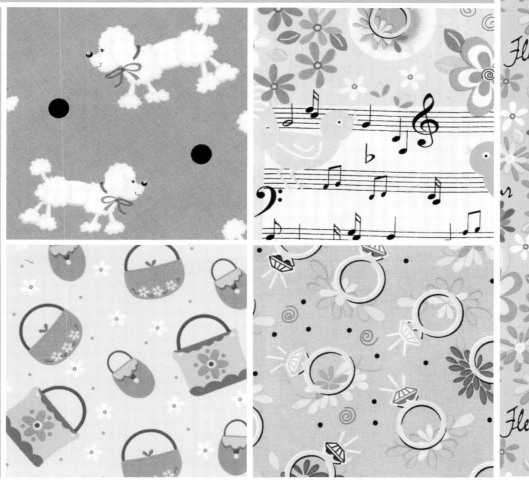

MEET DANA BROOKS

66 *Every day, every moment* in life is filled with excitement, passion, and experiences. Sometimes life takes us in a new, unexpected direction. The same is true of fabric. It's interesting what color, texture, and prints do to a quilter's life. They define moments. Turn an ordinary day into an extraordinary day, and a simple little dot into a fabulous polka dot. How easy is it to be fulfilled? It's really all about passion for the moments and memories created by quilting. 99

*I am a material girl...
living in a material world,
which is piled high with
color, style, fashion, and
texture. To turn it up a
notch, I add a touch of
animal-skin print!*

—Dana Brooks

Peppermint Twist Christmas Pillow
Designed and pieced by Dana Brooks
of My Lazy Daisy

Finished pillow size: 18" x 18"

Materials

Yardage is based on 42"-wide fabric, except where noted. Fat quarters measure 18" x 21" and fat eighths measure 9" x 21".

1 fat quarter of green print for yo-yos
1 fat eighth of red print for yo-yos
1 fat eighth of green stripe for border
1 fat eighth of dark-green print for border
1 fat eighth of brown solid for trunk
1 fat eighth of yellow solid for star
14" x 18" rectangle of white wool felt for pillow front
⅝ yard of green peppermint print for the pillow back
¼ yard of 72"-wide green tulle for the pillow edges
2¼ yards of red pom-pom trim for the pillow edges
1 yard of lime-green mini rickrack (³⁄₁₆" wide)
2 yards of red small rickrack (¾" wide)
1 red jingle bell
Embroidery floss in red and green
18" square pillow form

Cutting

From the white felt, cut:
1 rectangle, 12½" x 16½"

From the green print, cut:
18 circles, 4" diameter

From the red print, cut:
3 circles, 4" diameter

From the green stripe, cut:
2 strips, 1½" x 12½"
2 strips, 1½" x 18½"

From the dark-green print, cut:
2 strips, 2½" x 18½"

From the green peppermint print, cut:
1 square, 18½" x 18½"

Making the Yo-Yos

1 Turn ¼" to the wrong side around the edge of each 4" circle.

2 Using two strands of thread, hand sew a basting stitch along the folded edge. Pull the thread to gather the fabric, leaving a small circle open in the center. Make a few backstitches to secure the threads and tie a knot to finish, hiding the knot inside the gathers. Make 18 green and three red yo-yos.

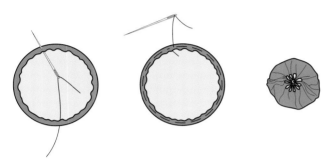

Appliquéing the Pillow Front

1 Using the patterns on page 95, prepare a brown trunk and a yellow star for your chosen appliqué method; the sample quilt features fusible appliqué with raw edges. The patterns are reversed for fusible appliqué.

Visit ShopMartingale.com/HowtoQuilt for free, downloadable instructions for a variety of appliqué techniques.

2 Referring to the pillow photo on page 92 for placement, arrange the trunk, star, and yo-yos on the felt rectangle.

3 Appliqué the trunk and star to the felt, temporarily removing yo-yos as necessary. Using red embroidery floss, sew a running stitch about ¼" inside each appliqué.

4 Using green or red thread, hand stitch each of the yo-yos to the felt around the outer edges.

5 Referring to the pillow photo and using green embroidery floss, sew a running stitch about ¼" outside the edges of the appliquéd shapes.

Assembling the Pillow Front

Stitch all pieces with right sides together and a ¼" seam allowance unless otherwise noted.

1 Baste the red rickrack to the edges of the appliquéd felt, positioning the center of the rickrack ¼" from the raw edges and overlapping the ends where the join will not be obvious. Trim the excess rickrack and set it aside for embellishment.

2 Sew green-striped 1½" x 12½" strips to the top and bottom edges of the felt, sandwiching the red rickrack between fabric layers. Press the seam allowances toward the green-striped strips.

3 Sew a green-striped 1½" x 18½" strip to each side of the pillow front. Press the seam allowances toward the green strips.

4 Sew a dark-green 2½" x 18½" strip to each side of the pillow front. Press the seam allowances toward the dark-green strips.

Finishing the Pillow

1 Cut the green tulle in half crosswise to make two strips, 4½" x 72". Fold each piece in half lengthwise and run a line of gathering stitches along the fold.

2 Position the folded tulle strips on the green peppermint-print square with the fold ⅛" from the raw edge and the bulk of the tulle lying toward the center of the pillow back. Overlap the ends of the tulle strips slightly. Pull the gathering stitches to fit the tulle to the pillow back, distributing the gathers evenly, and pin. Allow a little extra fullness in the gathers at each corner of the pillow.

SO, SO SIMPLE YO-YO

A large-size "Quick" Yo-Yo Maker from Clover makes it easy for you to produce the yo-yos for this project quickly. Just follow the manufacturer's instructions rather than cutting circles for the yo-yos.

3 Baste the red pom-pom trim on top of the tulle, centering the trim's header ¼" from the raw edges. Curve the header ends into the seam allowances to finish the raw edges.

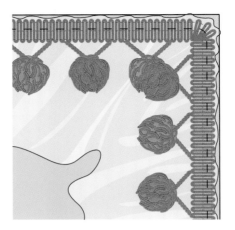

4 Place the pillow back on the pillow front, right sides together. Sew around all four sides, leaving an 8" opening for turning. Turn the pillow right side out.

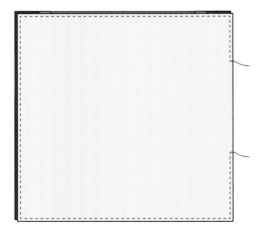

5 Make a loose bow from the leftover red rickrack and the lime rickrack. Hand stitch the bow and the jingle bell to the star as embellishment.

6 Insert the pillow form. Hand stitch the opening closed.

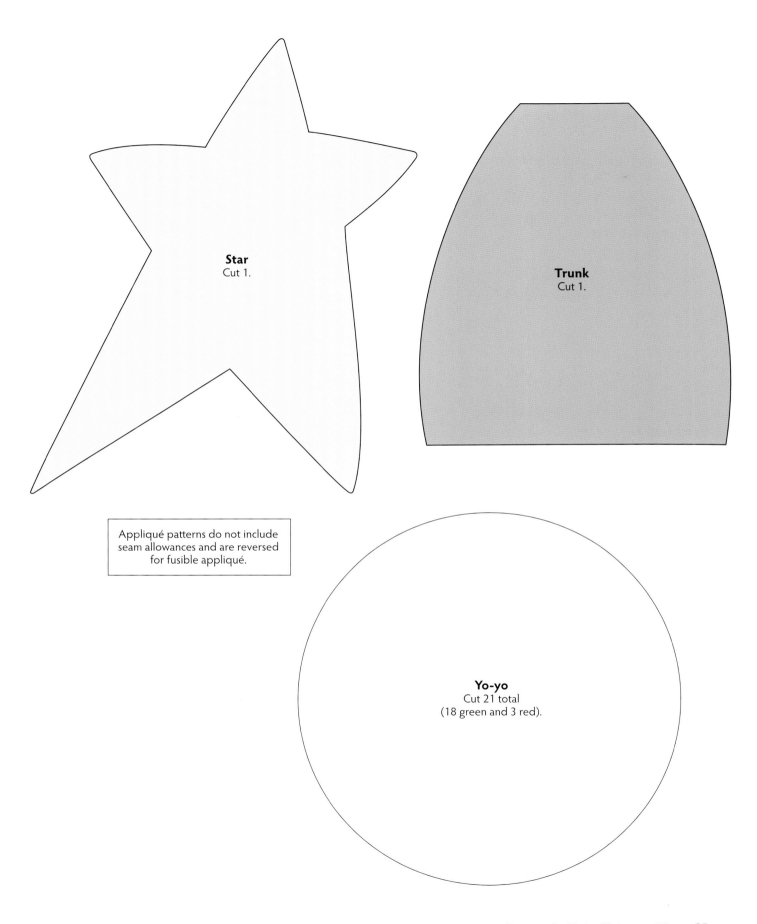

Star
Cut 1.

Trunk
Cut 1.

Appliqué patterns do not include
seam allowances and are reversed
for fusible appliqué.

Yo-yo
Cut 21 total
(18 green and 3 red).

Each of the contributors to this book is a fabric designer for Henry Glass. Learn a little more about the designers and their fabric collections at HenryGlassFabrics.com, and look for their fabrics at your local quilt shop.

Leanne Anderson
Website: www.TheWholeCountryCaboodle.com
Blog: TheWholeCountryCaboodle.blogspot.com

Dana Brooks
Website: www.MyLazyDaisy.com
Blog: MyLazyDaisy.blogspot.com

Linda Lum DeBono
Website: www.LindaLumDeBono.com
Blog: LindaLumDeBono.blogspot.com

Kim Diehl
Website: www.KimDiehl.com

Anni Downs
Website: www.HatchedandPatched.com.au
Blog: HatchedandPatched.typepad.com

Jill Finley
Website: www.JillilyStudio.com
Blog: JillilyStudio.blogspot.com

Amy Hamberlin
Blog: KatiCupcakeQuiltingCo.blogspot.com

Beth Hawkins and Elizabeth Hawkins
Website: www.LizzieBCre8ive.com
Blog: DreamLaughCreate.blogspot.com

Margot Languedoc
Website: www.ThePatternBasket.com
Blog: ThePatternBasket.blogspot.com

Little Quilts
Website: www.LittleQuilts.com
Blog: LittleQuilts.blogspot.com

Janet Nesbitt
Website: www.BuggyBarnQuilts.com

Vicki Oehlke
Website: www.WillowBerry-Lane.com
Blog: WillowBerryLane.wordpress.com

Heather Mulder Peterson
Website: www.AnkasTreasures.com
Blog: AnkasTreasures.wordpress.com

Jacquelynne Steves
Website: JacquelynneSteves.com
Blog: JacquelynneSteves.com/blog/